the GOOD life

the
GOOD
life

OVER 160 EASY, DELICIOUS RECIPES FOR A HEALTHY, LEAN LIFESTYLE

SALLY OBERMEDER
+ MAHA KORAIEM

ALLEN&UNWIN
SYDNEY · MELBOURNE · AUCKLAND · LONDON

First published in 2016

Allen & Unwin
83 Alexander Street
Crows Nest NSW 2065
Australia
Phone: (61 2) 8425 0100
Email: info@allenandunwin.com
Web: www.allenandunwin.com

Cataloguing-in-Publication details are available
from the National Library of Australia
www.trove.nla.gov.au

ISBN 978 1 76029 158 7

CUP AND TABLESPOON MEASURES: We have used Australian cup measures, of 250 ml (9 fl oz). Please note that the US and UK cup measures are slightly smaller, approximately 235 ml (7¾ fl oz). We have also used 20 ml (4 teaspoon) tablespoon measures. If you are using a 15 ml (3 teaspoon) tablespoon, add an extra teaspoon of the ingredient for each tablespoon specified.

OVEN GUIDE: For fan-forced ovens, as a general rule, set the oven temperature to 20°C (35°F) lower than indicated in the recipe.

Portraits of Sally and Maha: Peter Brew-Bevan

Recipe photographs: Joe Filshie

Styling and props: Georgie Dolling

Food preparation: Regina Walter

Copy editor: Melody Lord

Nutritional analysis: Chrissy Freer

Index: Puddingburn Publishing Services

Design by transformer.com.au
Set in 11/15 pt Chaparral Pro by transformer.com.au

Colour reproduction by Splitting Image Colour Studio Pty Ltd, Clayton, Victoria

Printed in China by C & C Offset Printing Co., Ltd.

10 9 8 7 6 5 4 3 2 1

CONTENTS

We are two sisters who love to eat and love to cook. We live different lives, but—like so many people—what we have in common is that we are busy and our time is stretched.

welcome

Despite this, we are firm believers in eating well, looking after ourselves and nourishing from the inside out.

Our love of delicious food connects us. We are constantly creating new recipes and swapping them with each other and with the readers of our lifestyle website, SWIISH.com.

A few years ago on SWIISH, we posted a picture of our 15-minute Prawn Curry in 'The SWIISH Kitchen' section of the site. We were flooded with comments and requests for more. From there, we continued to share our recipes with readers; at the basis of them all was our general food philosophy—it had to be lean, fab or fast.

Here is a bit of background: in 2011, Sal was diagnosed with Stage 3 breast cancer the day before giving birth to her daughter, Annabelle. The cancer was rare and extremely aggressive.

Following a torturous year of chemotherapy, radiation, a double mastectomy and numerous other surgeries, we got the good news that Sal was cancer-free. However, there was another challenge to face: Sal needed to rebuild her body, which had been particularly decimated by the treatment as well as affected by the usual strains and exhaustion that most women face during their first year of motherhood.

That's when green smoothies came into our lives. Sal had heard that they were great for your overall health, energy and wellbeing. She gave them a try and the results were pretty dramatic. The kilos came off easily, her skin glowed, her hair and nails grew stronger and her energy levels went through the roof.

At first we thought that it was perhaps because Sal was coming from such a low base, after having been through so much. But then Maha also adopted the green smoothie lifestyle and experienced similar results: loads more energy, significant weight loss, better sleep, and an all-round feeling of wellbeing. So we worked on creating new recipes together. The result? Our book, *Super Green Smoothies*. It's something that we are both incredibly passionate about and we're so proud of it.

The best part for us has been hearing, on a daily basis, how much it's changing the nutritional habits of people across Australia and in many other parts of the world (the US, UK, France, New Zealand, Canada, Mexico, Ireland and even Iceland, to name just a few) for the better. And it thrills us to know that people are feeling more energetic and becoming leaner and generally healthier by adding green smoothies to their diet.

Along with telling us how great they felt after adopting the *Super Green Smoothies* lifestyle, people kept asking us, 'What else do you eat each day? What does a day on a plate look like for you? What do you make for dinner? What are you serving up for your friends?' Which brings us

to this book. To be able to open up our kitchens and share our favourite recipes fills us with a huge amount of happiness.

You'll see that many of the recipes are focused on a super green lifestyle: fresh vegetables, fresh fruit, lean proteins and, of course, superfoods. All with the same philosophy: lean, fab or fast.

LEAN is all about how we like to live our life. Predominantly we work with The Good Life rule. It works on an 80/20 basis. So at least 80 per cent of the time we eat well and eat clean. Lean to us means flavour-filled, whole food that leaves you feeling full, satisfied and energised.

The rest of the time we go with the flow. Whether we're entertaining, celebrating or enjoying moments of splurging, we want more. We want it to be decadent, delicious and hit the spot. And that's okay. Because what is life without a little indulgence? Speaking of which, see our Berrylicious Meringue recipe on page 222 ... how FAB!

FAST meals are our midweek specialty. Juggling jobs, a website, a business, a growing team, kids, family, friends and charity commitments means that we have to think smart about maximum taste and nutrition for minimum effort and time. Just because it's quick should

never mean it's tasteless. It should never be a choice between taste and time.

For us, life is all about balance, and cooking is all about love. It feels good to nurture our bodies with clean, lean, whole food. We believe the kitchen is at the heart of every home. It's where meals are cooked; where conversation is enjoyed; where entertaining happens; where drinks get spilled; and where memories are made.

We hope that this book helps you to feel good, to love food and, like us, to make special memories for yourself, with your family and friends. After all, that is the good life.

Sally xx Maha

what is
lean, fab, fast?

Our food philosophy—LEAN, FAB, FAST—is really a reflection of who we are, and our means of trying to achieve health and balance in our busy lives.

What we've learned over the years is that the better we are at looking after ourselves, and at nurturing ourselves from the inside out, the more we are able to be healthy, happy and present as a parent, partner, sister, daughter, friend, employee and SWIISH.com girlboss.

What can seem like a small action, such as choosing to eat a healthy breakfast instead of skipping it, ends up having a big impact. It sets the tone for the day and helps us make other positive choices, such as deciding to exercise, or go to bed a little earlier, or reach for a healthy, clean-eating snack instead of processed foods.

But we're not perfect. We don't always get it right. And that's okay. That's part of what balance is. It's about doing what you can, in the time you have, to look after yourself as best you can.

We've labelled each recipe in this book to help you: the recipes labelled LEAN and FAST are there for your everyday enjoyment. LEAN recipes are lower in kilojoules (calories) but high on taste—so they are the perfect choice for anyone who is looking to lose weight or keep it lean.

FAST meals are super delicious and on the table in next to no time. Often 'fast' is mistaken for 'boring', but these recipes are full of flavour, superfoods, proteins and leafy greens as well as quick to make—perfect for busy days.

The FAB recipes are fine as part of our balanced approach ... for those times you want to indulge a little, impress your friends or feel like spending a bit more time in the kitchen. Some recipes can be lean and fast, or fab and fast. You'll see them labelled this way at the top of each recipe.

Ultimately, LEAN, FAB, FAST is about feeling good and having fun—living the good life. As we like to say, it's about having your cake and eating it too—just not the whole cake!

LEAN

FAB

FAST

THE GOOD LIFE RULE

What is The Good Life rule, you ask? Put simply, it's a philosophy we've adopted where most of the time, about 80 per cent, we eat clean, lean, whole foods. The other 20 per cent of the time is when we're entertaining friends with a decadent dessert, grabbing a pizza or we're on holidays and indulging in the local cuisine without guilt.

The Good Life philosophy is a lifestyle, not a fad diet where we deny ourselves carbs or don't get to eat chocolate. It's about being balanced, listening to what our bodies need and eating mainly lean proteins, lots of leafy greens and superfoods.

The more you stick to this and choose foods that are predominantly unprocessed, you will get lean, feel great and look fabulous.

So, 80 per cent of the time, we suggest you choose recipes marked as LEAN. For the other 20 per cent, go ahead and be FAB. Just make sure you invite us over when you make Mum's incredible chocolate tart (see page 267).

♡

SUPERFOODS

Superfoods are everywhere these days! You can't go online, pick up a newspaper or walk through a shopping centre without seeing a chia-sprinkled quinoa brekkie bowl or a kale-and-goji-berry smoothie. Everyone seems to be obsessed (us included!).

Unlike some other health trends, however, superfoods aren't a passing fad. These amazing ingredients are what we like to call nutrient 'powerhouses', packed full of just about as much nourishment as you can get. They contain vitamins, minerals, antioxidants and so much more.

The reason we love them so much is because of the incredible health benefits that everyone can experience by adding superfoods to their diets. We're talking increased energy, improved digestion, clearer skin, better sleep and even reduced stress, just to name a few. Adding superfoods to your daily diet can even help reduce the risk of chronic disease so that you can live a healthier life.

The best part though? They can taste amazing! Especially if you cook with them the right way. That's why we've made sure our recipes are full of superfood goodness for everyone to enjoy.

Don't know your matcha from your maca? Here's a rundown of some of our favourite superfoods.

Acai

The acai berry is a purply, reddish fruit that you can buy in the form of raw berries, powders or tablets. It was deemed a superfood after studies suggested that the fruit pulp was even richer in antioxidants than raspberries, blackberries, cranberries, strawberries and blueberries! It's also full of fibre and healthy fats and seriously delicious. A lot of people describe the taste as something between a rich raspberry or blackberry and a piece of dark chocolate. Yum!

Agave nectar

Agave nectar is a great natural alternative to sugar because it is not only tastier, it's a lot healthier too. Agave nectar is a liquid made from a cactus-like plant native to Mexico and South Africa. Its key health-promoting property is that it has a naturally low glycaemic index (GI), which means you get all that sweetness without the blood sugar spike.

Chia

Chia seeds are probably one of the most commonly used superfoods, and for good reason. With a huge amount of omega-3, calcium and potassium, these tiny little guys are among the most powerful superfoods out there. They also expand in your stomach, making you feel full for longer, so they can be the perfect addition to your morning smoothie or brekkie bowl!

Chlorophyll

Unlike the other foods on this list, chlorophyll isn't a fruit, seed or vegetable. Instead, it's the green pigment in leafy greens that helps plants to carry out photosynthesis. But that's not all it's good for. Chlorophyll is said to encourage healing in your body, promote cleansing, relieve swelling, help control body odour and even keep hunger cravings at bay. It's usually found in a liquid form, making it the perfect addition to your green smoothies or even water.

Coconut milk

Not only is coconut milk delicious, it's also really good for you and can be used in so many different ways. Unlike normal milk, coconut milk is lactose-free so it's great for anyone with an intolerance (it's a favourite

among vegans too). Rich and creamy, it makes the perfect base for milkshakes, smoothies, yoghurt and even ice cream! But it's important to note that coconut milk does contain a high amount of fat compared with normal milk. That's why we opt for coconut milks that are blended with rice or almond milk (available in cartons from the supermarket)—still providing a delicious taste, but less fat for the body.

Coconut oil

Extracted from the meat of a coconut, coconut oil not only helps to keep you full but is also said to increase your energy expenditure so that you burn more fat. It does wonders for your skin and hair too.

Coconut water

This low-kJ, all-natural health drink is packed with electrolytes and minerals that fuel your body with essential nutrients and help keep you extra hydrated. A much better option than reaching for soft drinks, as well as a fabulous addition to your smoothie.

Fermented and cultured foods

Fermented and cultured foods can be found in the form of pickles, kimchi, kefir and sauerkraut. Don't be fooled by the off-putting name: these foods can be seriously yummy! Plus, they make your belly happy. Fermented and cultured foods may promote the growth of beneficial bacteria in the gut, resulting in better digestion and a clearer elimination system. They make you feel better, lighter, leaner, cleaner. Oh, and you get a flatter tummy. Win!

Goji berries

These nutritionally dense berries are native to the Himalayas. Although only relatively new to the western world, they have been used for thousands of years in Tibet and China. With high levels of vitamin C, fibre and amino acids, goji berries also have the highest concentration of protein in any fruit.

Kale

Kale has got to be top of the list when it comes to superpowered greens. This dark green leafy vegetable is a source of vitamins A, C and K, along with minerals such as calcium, potassium and folate. Aside from antioxidants, kale has enough fibre to help bind bile acids and lower blood cholesterol levels to reduce the risk of heart disease, especially when it's cooked. It's also super-versatile. We love using it in smoothies, pesto, soup, salads and even to make chips!

Kefir

Basically, kefir is fermented milk made from kefir 'grains'. They're not really grains but they have a similar lumpy texture. Although it tastes a bit like yoghurt, kefir has around five times the probiotic nutrients. It also contains calcium, biotin, folate, magnesium, enzymes and vitamins K2 and B12. What does that mean for you? Detoxification, a stronger immune system and stronger bones, fewer allergies and improved digestion. And it's delish. Add it to smoothies, oats or desserts, as you would yoghurt.

Maca

We are mad about maca! This powdered plant root is full of vitamins B, C and E, as well as iron, phosphorus, calcium, zinc, magnesium and essential amino acids. If you suffer from cramps, body pain, mood swings, depression or anxiety, this may be the superfood for you. Maca is said to help regulate hormones and boost your mood. Yay! With a bit of a malted, oaty kind of flavour, maca is the perfect addition to a smoothie, brekkie bowl or dessert.

Matcha

It may look just like green dust, but there's more to it than meets the eye. Made of ground up green tea leaves, matcha is rich in antioxidants called polyphenols, which have been said to help with blood pressure reduction, blood sugar regulation, anti-ageing and even protection against cancer and heart disease. Not to mention, it gives your metabolism a major boost. Double win!

Quinoa

This grain-like seed has rocked the health-food world, and for good reason! Not only does it contain good stuff like essential fatty acids, proteins, antioxidants and heart-healthy fats, its grain-like consistency makes it a super healthy alternative to dinner-time staples such as pasta and rice, as it is rich in protein, which leaves you feeling fuller for longer.

Raw cacao

Unlike the cocoa in most chocolate, raw cacao is made by cold-pressing unroasted cocoa beans. This removes the fat from the beans and keeps all the living enzymes intact. Raw cacao is an amazing antioxidant that can help to repair the damage caused by free radicals and may even reduce the risk of cardiovascular disease and cancer. In fact, there are so many antioxidants in raw cacao that they make up

10 per cent of its weight. With the addition of oil and sweetener, cacao has a very chocolatey taste, making it perfect for both smoothies and desserts!

Spirulina

Spirulina is made up of plant-like organisms that are full of iron, protein and beta-carotene as well as vitamins B and K. Some of the health benefits may include liver cancer and heart disease prevention, improved mood, protection against allergic reactions, increased energy and metabolic rate, lowered cholesterol and improved digestion. It usually comes dried or freeze-dried so you can just chomp on it if you want ... but we recommend blending it in a smoothie.

Turmeric

This bright orange spice shouldn't be restricted to curries. Packed full of flavour and a whole lot of health benefits, turmeric is perfect for all sorts of dishes. It's great in winter recipes due to its amazing ability to help with the symptoms of the flu. It's also commonly deemed a 'natural aspirin' because of its anti-inflammatory properties that help to relieve the pain and swelling caused by injuries or headaches. Turmeric is even said to help fight free radicals that damage the skin and make it lose its elasticity. Sounds good to us!

PREP YOUR PANTRY

The road to a healthy lifestyle begins in the kitchen. More specifically, in your pantry. Stocking up on superfoods and other nutritious ingredients is the easiest way to curb that sneaky snacking routine—we've all been there!

While we do like to mix it up when it comes to our recipes, there are always going to be a few ingredients that will be used over and over again. We've decided to make things just a little bit simpler for you with our pantry 'essentials' list. Whether you're whipping up a meal from scratch or simply wanting to add a little extra flavour or a superfood boost, these handy essentials will be there to back you up.

Almond meal

Almond meal is a fantastic, low-carb alternative to real flour because it's high in protein and good fats, and is free of gluten. You can buy it from the supermarket, or make your own by processing almonds to a powder and storing it in an airtight container in the fridge.

Apple cider vinegar

This tangy liquid is a definite must-have for your pantry. Not only does it make a great addition to marinades, dressings and sauces, it's amazing for your health too. Apple cider vinegar can help to lower blood sugar and insulin levels, which may help delay the effects of ageing and promote weight loss. We recommend drinking a teaspoon or two mixed with a glass of water every morning.

Brown rice

We like to substitute brown rice for white rice when we can. It has a lovely chewy texture that just seems to go well with everything! It's also high in complex carbohydrates and full of hunger-busting fibre.

Cacao powder

Most people who like to bake have a box of cocoa in their cupboard, but if you want to up the nutritional value then try cacao powder instead. It's perfect for adding that yummy, chocolatey taste to smoothies, snacks and desserts.

Chia seeds

We've already mentioned the amazing health benefits of these little seeds, so they had to make it onto our essentials list. You can use them in many different breakfast, dessert and snack recipes.

Coconut oil

Coconut oil is our favourite alternative to regular oil, and for good reason! It's rich in essential fatty acids, it's great for your hair and skin, and it can be used in just about any recipe. It also tastes great!

Dark chocolate

We consider dark chocolate healthier than regular chocolate because of its higher cocoa content, making it richer in antioxidants and lower in sugar: the more cocoa, the better. We always love to have at least one sweet treat in the house for when our sugar cravings kick in!

Flaxseed meal

Like almond meal, flaxseed is a great filler for foods like bread, cakes and cookies. It's an amazing source of minerals, fibre and omega-3 fatty acids. To get the most out of the seeds, they need to be ground up. That's why flaxseed meal is so great!

the GOOD *life*

Herbs and spices

Put simply, herbs and spices are the key to adding maximum flavour to any dish. Not to mention, most of them are quite high in antioxidants, and the hotter kinds of spices in particular can help speed up your metabolism. Cinnamon and nutmeg are our favourites when it comes to making sweeter dishes, while turmeric, coriander, cumin, rosemary and basil are go-tos for curries and soups!

Norbu

Also known as monk fruit sugar, this natural sweetener has 96 per cent fewer kilojoules (calories) than white sugar. Like stevia, it doesn't impact on insulin or blood sugar levels.

Nuts

Nuts are full of healthy fats that help you feel full, making them the perfect snack to keep in your pantry. Almonds are our favourite because they're one of the lower kilojoule (calorie) options, and they taste delicious when roasted and sprinkled with a bit of tamarind and sea salt.

Oats

Oats can be used in so many different ways. Cook them for breakfast, use them to make cookies, or even grind them into flour! They're rich in complex carbohydrates and taste absolutely delicious.

Quinoa

This grain-like seed is a must-have for any healthy pantry. It's the perfect high protein, gluten-free alternative to your usual pasta and rice. Believe it or not, you can even use it to make porridge! It tastes amazing.

Rice malt syrup

This is one that pops up in a lot of our recipes. That's because it's probably the healthiest sugar-swap you can get. Made from 100 per cent organic brown rice, this sweet syrup is high in complex carbohydrates and completely fructose-free. It's fantastic for sweetening up breakfasts, desserts, honeycomb and caramel.

Stevia

If you're trying to cut down on sugar in your diet, you have to keep some of this in the house (or in your handbag for that coffee on the go). Stevia is an all-natural, zero-kilojoule (-calorie) substitute for sugar. It's also a lot sweeter, so you don't have to use as much.

FRIDGE & FREEZER

As some of our fellow *Super Green Smoothies* sippers may well know, we love our fruits and vegies! We prefer to use them frozen for our smoothies because it helps to reduce prep time, cuts down on waste (rather than throwing out fruit and vegies that are overripe), and also because those fruity flavours really pop when they're colder.

But when it comes to food recipes, things are a bit different (nobody wants to eat a frozen salad!). Our recipes call for produce that is both fresh and frozen. Keep your fridge or freezer stocked full of these delicious, nutritious ingredients and you'll never be short of a good meal!

Avocados

Who doesn't love an avo? This creamy fruit is full of healthy fats, which are great for your hair, skin and nails. Avocados can be eaten with eggs, in salads, on sandwiches or as a healthier alternative to butter.

Baby spinach

This has to be one of our favourite leafy green vegies! It's full of all the vitamins and minerals you need to increase vitality, restore energy and improve the quality of your blood. It's also extremely versatile as it can be used in just about any meal. We love to keep some fresh and some frozen.

Bananas

We love bananas because they're the ultimate energy food. They're also rich in potassium, which is an essential mineral for maintaining healthy blood pressure and heart function. You shouldn't keep bananas in the fridge though. The reason we've put them in this section is because you should always have some frozen! There's no better way to make healthy ice cream than to blend up a few frozen bananas.

Berries

We eat berries pretty much every day. It's a good idea to keep some in the fridge and some frozen. The fresh ones can be used as a garnish on a dessert or brekkie bowl, while the frozen ones are perfect for smoothies and our Fro-Yo Bark 4 Ways on page 226 (trust us, you want to try it). Berries are also rich in antioxidants, so eat up!

Broccoli

We all know broccoli is one of the healthiest foods out there, so it's always good to have on hand. With dietary fibre, minerals and vitamins A, B and E, it's the perfect way to supercharge any meal. We like to keep a little in the fridge and a little in the freezer.

Cauliflower

Cauliflower is super-handy because it can be used as a substitute for pizza bases and rice (we have recipes for both in this book!). The only difference is that it's low-carb and full of nutrients like omega-3 fatty acids, choline, fibre, manganese, biotin and phosphorus. Always keep cauliflower in your fridge so it maintains its freshness.

Cheese

A little bit of feta goes a long way! Haloumi is always a must-have too. They both work with salads, eggs, on toasties and just on their own.

the GOOD *life*

Coconut water

We like to keep coconut water handy to use in smoothies or even just to drink on its own. Again, look for a version that contains no added sugar.

Eggs

Packed full of vitamins, minerals, high-quality proteins and good fats, eggs are like little nutrition powerhouses. An egg is also the one ingredient that seems to turn up in breakfast, lunch, dinner and dessert! So it's a good idea to have them handy.

Fermented and cultured foods

If you have poor digestion, fermented and cultured foods are going to be your new best friend. They promote the growth of healthy bacteria in the gut, which results in better digestion and a clearer elimination system. You can find these foods in the form of pickles, kimchi, kefir, kombucha (see below) and sauerkraut (see page 5).

Fresh herbs

Herbs are a must-have for any kitchen. They're perfect for adding a tonne of flavour to meals. We like to keep ours in the fridge, but keeping some in the freezer will help them last longer. Try chopping some up and freezing them in an ice-cube tray with a little water or oil. They're perfect to throw in the pot when you're making curries, sauces or soups.

Kombucha

Kombucha is a fermented tea-based drink that is made using SCOBY (symbiotic culture of bacteria and yeast). It may not sound appealing, but it's actually delicious! This healthy, probiotic beverage is usually sweet and sparkling. It's the perfect alternative to soft drinks.

Medjool dates

Medjool dates are our choice because they're super sweet and soft, compared to others that can be bland and dry. They're also very high in fibre, which helps you feel full for longer. You can use dates in brekkie bowls, smoothies, desserts and even to make a substitute for caramel! They hit the spot and are the perfect healthy snack to keep in your fridge.

Non-dairy milk

Plant-based milk isn't just for vegans and the lactose intolerant. Soy milk is high in protein, and almond milk is low in kilojoules (calories). These are all great alternatives to use in baking. Hazelnut milk is full of vitamin B, and coconut milk is rich in vitamins, minerals and fibre; both are great as a substitute for thin (pouring) cream due to their similar consistency. Be sure to read the labels though and pick one without added sugars and flavours.

Tahini

This one's not as common as the others but it definitely should be. Tahini is an oily paste made from finely ground sesame seeds. It's full of vitamins and is a richer source of protein than milk, sunflower seeds, soya beans and most nuts. It's great for making your own hummus, drizzled on a salad or even on toast!

Yoghurt

One thing we always have in our fridge is a tub of good-quality yoghurt. It's perfect for breakfast, as a snack, or even as a substitute for cream in a dessert. Not to mention, it's seriously good for you too! Yoghurt can be full of live, active cultures that help to balance the microflora in your intestines and keep your tummy happy.

SUPER SWAPS

Imagine a place where cakes, cookies and slices were actually healthy … Welcome to our world! We believe that you can have your cake and eat it too.

In many recipes in this book, we have swapped certain flours, sugars and other pantry regulars for clean, natural alternatives. That's because many of those flours and sugars can be laden with processed ingredients and additives that aren't healthy or may make you feel tired, sluggish and bloated.

It's not a massive deal if you don't want to swap. But if you can, it's just one more step towards giving your body the goodness it needs as well as the chance to process what you're eating more easily, leaving you feeling lean and energetic.

Butter

Swap for: coconut oil; organic butter

Organic butter, made from the milk of cows that are not given synthetic growth or breeding hormones, is as nutrient dense as regular butter, while coconut oil is great for energy and can help to burn fat.

Dairy milk

Swap for: almond milk; soy milk; coconut milk; rice milk

Cow's milk contains lactose that doesn't always agree with everyone's digestive system. Try using one of the alternatives instead for a lower kilojoule, lactose-free, vegan option.

Flour

Swap for: coconut flour; buckwheat flour; chickpea flour (besan); almond meal

Flour is used in so many different recipes, but ordinary white flour doesn't have much nutritional value. Try substituting one of these healthier options to supercharge your cakes and slices!

Soft drinks

Swap for: kombucha; infused water; coconut water

We all know that soft drinks are no match for other water but sometimes water can get a bit dull. Try a ginger and lemon kombucha if you like ginger ale, or infuse your water with berries; sliced lemons, limes or oranges; or even cucumber and basil instead.

Sugar

Swap for: stevia; agave syrup; norbu; rice malt syrup; raw honey; xylitol or erythritol

The problem with sugar is that it has a high glycaemic index (GI), meaning it gives a short-lived energy surge that later results in a major crash. It also is high in kilojoules (calories), which can lead to weight gain. Try one of the alternatives instead.

Vegetable oil

Swap for: coconut oil; almond oil; macadamia oil; olive oil

Common vegetable oils often contain omega-6 polyunsaturated fatty acids, which can be harmful to your body when consumed in excess. Not only are these oil swaps safe for your health, they're actually good for it!

White bread

Swap for: dark rye bread; sourdough bread; broccoli bread; sprouted grain bread

the GOOD Life

Much like white flour and pasta, white bread isn't very nutrient dense. It can also contain hidden sugars that aren't great for your teeth (or your waistline)! The alternatives will help you get the most out of your sandwich.

White rice

Swap for: brown rice; black rice; quinoa; cauliflower rice

Rice is pretty much an essential accompaniment to any Asian-style dish. However, white rice has a higher glycaemic index (GI) than the alternatives and may cause a spike in your blood sugar levels. Try one of these low-GI, high-fibre swaps instead, or choose cauliflower rice for a low-kJ, low-carb option.

MEAL PLANS

You'll see that towards the end of *The Good Life* (page 270), we've pulled together some suggested weekly meal plans for you. Not only does planning ahead make life that little bit easier but, by following these, you'll be getting a huge range of nutrients thanks to the lean proteins, superfoods and vegies in each recipe. Plus we have included dessert every day! We can hear you rejoicing from here! The daily kilojoule (calorie) count comes in at around 6276 kilojoules (1500 calories), including dessert. If you are on a weight-loss diet and/or want to skip dessert, then most days come in under 5020 kilojoules (1200 calories). Either way, you're getting flavour-filled meals full of goodness. Enjoy!

FREQUENTLY ASKED QUESTIONS

Are these recipes paleo?

Yes, quite a lot of them are! A paleo diet is full of fresh, unprocessed foods but avoids dairy, legumes, grains, processed foods and refined sugar—all very much in line with The Good Life philosophy. Look for recipes marked paleo or P at the top of the page.

Are they sugar-free?

Yes, many of the recipes in *The Good Life* contain no refined sugar, such as white sugar, which causes an insulin spike and impacts on blood glucose levels. Sugar-free recipes are labelled sugar-free or SF. There are plenty of sweet treats in this book, but we prefer to use natural sweeteners, such as rice malt syrup or stevia. We also use maple syrup and honey, which are paleo-friendly.

Then why do some recipes list sugar?

Well, while we want you to try to eat clean so you feel as good as you possibly can, not everyone is quite there yet. Ultimately, we want to encourage you to use the cleaner options, not intimidate you. You'll find that using these clean sugar swaps will still make each recipe taste amazing but be good for you too.

We also understand that these newer options can seem expensive or hard to find. The good news is that most, if not all, are available from supermarkets or health food stores. They might cost a little bit more but we believe that it's better to invest in good health now, and live the best life that you can.

How healthy are the FAB dishes?

Most of them are extremely healthy. Take our Super Filling Brunch Bowl, for example—it is choc-a-block full of protein and healthy fats like avocado, nuts and coconut oil as well as low-GI quinoa. It's sugar-free and packed with green goodness but it's higher in kilojoules (calories) because it's so nutrient-dense.

On the dessert front, most of the FAB dishes, such as Berrylicious Meringue, fall into The Good Life rule and should be seen as treats rather than everyday foods. If, like Sally, you want a daily sweet treat, then the LEAN desserts make a great choice.

What does 'alkaline' mean?

Basically, alkaline is the internal state in which your immune system, your cells and all the chemical reactions inside them are working with maximum efficiency. Your body is said to be at its healthiest when your insides are working in an alkaline environment, as opposed to an acidic one.

Am I alkaline?

The level of alkalinity versus acidity in your body is measured by a pH value, with 4.5 being very acidic and 9.5 being highly alkaline. You want to be around a 7.

What should I eat to be more alkaline?

The fastest way to get alkaline is to up your daily vegie intake as much as you can. Dieticians recommend you eat about 5–7 servings of vegetables daily. Enjoy a smoothie plus one of our superfood salads or smoothie brekkie bowls each day and you'll knock this goal right out of the park!

breakfast

TURKISH EGGS WITH SUMAC YOGHURT

GLUTEN-FREE | NUT-FREE | SUGAR-FREE | VEGETARIAN | 1096 KJ/262 CAL PER SERVE

2 tablespoons olive oil, plus 2 teaspoons extra to serve

2 garlic cloves, finely chopped

½ teaspoon cumin seeds

½ red (Spanish) onion, finely diced

1 large red capsicum (pepper), seeded and finely chopped

2 long green chillies, seeded and finely chopped

2–3 vine-ripened tomatoes, finely chopped, or use a 400 g (14 oz) tin of diced tomatoes

45 g (1½ oz/1 cup) baby spinach leaves

4 eggs (free-range, organic)

handful of flat-leaf (Italian) parsley, chopped

½ lemon, to serve

crusty bread, to serve (optional)

Sumac yoghurt

75 g (2¾ oz/¼ cup) Greek-style yoghurt

½ teaspoon minced garlic

large pinch of ground sumac

1 tablespoon olive oil

1 teaspoon lemon juice

Preheat the oven to 180°C (350°F).

Heat the olive oil in a heavy-based frying pan or skillet over medium heat. Add the garlic and cumin seeds and fry until aromatic. Add the onion, capsicum and green chillies, frying gently until softened. Add the tomatoes, mix everything together well and season with salt and pepper to taste. Leave it to bubble away for about 10 minutes or until the mixture starts to thicken.

Meanwhile, make the sumac yoghurt. Mix the yoghurt, garlic, sumac, olive oil and lemon juice in a large serving bowl and whisk together gently. Season with salt and pepper to taste and set aside.

When the tomato mixture has cooked, add the baby spinach and stir until the spinach wilts.

Divide the tomato and spinach mixture between 4 ovenproof ramekins. Make a hollow in the mixture in each ramekin. Crack one egg into a cup and carefully pour it into one of the hollows. Repeat with the remaining eggs until all the hollows have been filled. Stand the ramekins on a baking tray and bake them for 10 minutes or until the eggs are cooked to your liking (we like to cook them until the egg whites are just opaque but the yolks are still runny).

Remove from the oven, drizzle with extra olive oil and sprinkle with the chopped parsley. Serve immediately, with half a lemon, a side of bread and the sumac yoghurt.

SERVES 4

SUPER FILLING BRUNCH BOWL

DAIRY-FREE | GLUTEN-FREE | SUGAR-FREE | VEGETARIAN | 3343 KJ/799 CAL PER SERVE

50 g (1¾ oz/¼ cup) quinoa, uncooked

30 g (1 oz/½ cup) broccoli, chopped into small florets

small bunch of asparagus, ends discarded, stems chopped into 3 cm (1¼ inch) pieces

50 g (1¾ oz/2 cups) kale ribbons (stalks removed, leaves sliced)

45 g (1½ oz/1 cup) baby spinach leaves

small handful of mint leaves

small handful of coriander (cilantro) leaves

small handful of flat-leaf (Italian) parsley leaves

4 eggs (free-range, organic)

1 avocado, halved, peeled, stone removed

15 g (½ oz/⅛ cup) shelled pistachio nuts

For the dressing

juice and zest of 1 lemon

½ teaspoon ground turmeric

80 ml (2¾ fl oz/⅓ cup) melted coconut oil

tip Because this dish is so nutrient-dense, we typically have it as a brekkie/lunch combo.

Cook quinoa according to packet instructions and set aside. Put the ingredients for the dressing in a small bowl and whisk them together until well combined and the colour begins to darken to a warm orange.

Next, wash the broccoli, asparagus, kale, spinach and herbs. Set aside.

Bring a large saucepan of water to the boil, then lower the heat slightly to a constant simmer. Add the eggs in their shells and cook for 5–6 minutes (you'll get a runny yolk at 5 minutes and a more firmly set yolk at 6 minutes. We like to split the difference at 5½ minutes).

Once the eggs are cooked, remove them from the pan and submerge them in a bowl of cold water. Allow to stand for a few minutes to cool, then remove the shells and set the eggs aside.

Place the broccoli and asparagus in a microwave-safe bowl, adding a small amount of water and using a plate to cover the bowl. Microwave for 2 minutes on High. Remove and drain off any excess water.

Heat a nonstick frying pan over high heat and put the washed kale, spinach and herbs into the hot pan. Slowly add the dressing, stirring constantly. Remove the pan from the heat as soon as the leaves have wilted and absorbed the dressing: watch carefully so that you don't overcook them.

Divide the quinoa, broccoli, asparagus, greens, avocado and eggs between two bowls and serve, sprinkled with pistachios.

SERVES 2

LEMON & THYME HALOUMI ON OLIVE SOURDOUGH

NUT-FREE | SUGAR-FREE | VEGETARIAN | 1648 KJ/394 CAL PER SERVE

400 g (14 oz) haloumi cheese

4 slices olive sourdough bread

1 tablespoon olive oil

4 thyme sprigs (or 1 teaspoon dried thyme), leaves picked

1 lemon, halved, to serve

Cut the haloumi in half lengthways, then slice it into 1 cm (⅜ inch) thick slices. Toast the olive sourdough and transfer to a serving plate.

Meanwhile, heat the olive oil in a frying pan over medium–high heat and fry the haloumi slices 2 minutes on each side or until a light golden brown in colour.

Transfer the fried haloumi to a serving plate and sprinkle with the sprigs of thyme and a squeeze of lemon. Serve with the sourdough and enjoy.

SERVES 4

3-INGREDIENT SCRAMBLED EGGS

GLUTEN-FREE | NUT-FREE | SUGAR-FREE | VEGETARIAN | 1385 KJ/331 CAL PER SERVE

4 eggs (free-range, organic)

250 g (9 oz/1 punnet) sweet cherry tomatoes (optional, to serve)

2 teaspoons butter, for frying

1½ long red chillies, seeded and finely chopped

100 g (3½ oz) goat's or Danish feta cheese, crumbled (or finely chopped)

Crack the eggs into a small bowl and use a fork to whisk. Season with a small amount of salt (remember that the feta is salty) and some pepper.

Wash and halve the cherry tomatoes, season with a little salt and pepper and set aside.

Heat a small knob of butter in a frying pan over medium heat. Add the chilli and feta, stirring gently with a wooden spoon to combine. As the feta begins to soften, add the eggs and gently stir with a wooden spoon until just scrambled and cooked through.

Remove from the heat and serve immediately with the cherry tomatoes.

SERVES 2

GOING NUTS GRANOLA

DAIRY-FREE | GLUTEN-FREE | PALEO | SUGAR-FREE | VEGAN | 1226 KJ/293 CAL PER SERVE

155 g (5½ oz/1 cup) raw cashews

160 g (5¾ oz/1 cup) raw almonds

40 g (1½ oz/¼ cup) brazil nuts

25 g (1 oz/¼ cup) pecan nuts

40 g (1½ oz/¼ cup) sunflower seeds

40 g (1½ oz/¼ cup) pepitas (pumpkin seeds)

20 g (¾ oz/¼ cup) shredded coconut

60 ml (2 fl oz/¼ cup) coconut oil

1 teaspoon natural vanilla extract or vanilla bean paste

125 ml (4 fl oz/½ cup) rice malt syrup

Preheat the oven to 135°C (270°F). Line a baking tray with baking paper and set aside.

In a blender or food processor, put the cashews, almonds, brazil nuts, pecans, sunflower seeds, pepitas and shredded coconut. Pulse until the mixture has broken up into smaller pieces.

In a medium saucepan over medium–high heat, combine the coconut oil, natural vanilla extract (or vanilla bean paste, if using) and rice malt syrup and stir to combine. When melted and well combined, add the nut mixture and stir well to ensure that the nuts are all evenly coated.

Spread the nut mixture evenly across the prepared baking tray. Bake for about 20 minutes or until the mixture is lightly browned. Remove from the oven and set aside. When the granola has hardened, break it up into pieces and store in an airtight container. It should last for up to 5 days.

SERVES 12

FAB FAST

FUL MEDAMES

DAIRY-FREE | GLUTEN-FREE | NUT-FREE | SUGAR-FREE | VEGAN | 1992 KJ/476 CAL PER SERVE

3 tablespoons olive oil, plus 5 ml extra to serve

400 g (14 oz) tin broad (fava) beans (found in International aisle of supermarkets or at delis or Middle Eastern grocers)

1 garlic clove, minced

1 teaspoon ground cumin

pinch of cayenne pepper (optional)

1–2 tablespoons fresh lemon juice

2 tomatoes, cut into 1 cm (³/₈ inch) dice

7 g (¼ oz/¼ cup) chopped flat-leaf (Italian) parsley

1 Lebanese (short) cucumber, diced

¼ red (Spanish) onion, diced

5 pickled turnips (available at delis), cut into 1 cm dice

5 g (⅕ oz/¼ cup) fresh mint leaves, to serve

1 lemon, cut into wedges, to serve

Lebanese bread or flatbread, to serve (optional)

Heat 2 tablespoons of the olive oil in a medium saucepan over medium heat. Add half of the beans, including the liquid from the can, garlic, cumin, cayenne (if using) and lemon juice. Mash the remaining beans roughly with a fork, then add to the mixture.

Stir well for around 5 minutes or until the mixture thickens. If it's looking too dry, add another tablespoon of olive oil. Remove from heat.

Combine the tomato and parsley in a small serving bowl and drizzle with a tiny bit of olive oil.

In a separate bowl, mix together the cucumber and red onion.

Serve ful medames immediately with tomato, cucumber salad, pickled turnips, mint, lemon wedges and bread (if using).

SERVES 2

tips
• We don't think you need to add any salt as there is usually salt in the tin of beans, but you may add salt to taste.
• Try serving ful medames with boiled or fried eggs.

BANANA BREAD

DAIRY-FREE | SUGAR-FREE | VEGETARIAN | 778 KJ/186 CAL PER SERVE

70 g (2½ oz/½ cup) wholemeal self-raising flour

50 g (1¾ oz/½ cup) almond meal

60 g (2 oz/½ cup) vanilla protein powder

20 g (¾ oz/¼ cup) shredded coconut

¼ teaspoon ground cinnamon

3 large, overripe bananas (almost black), peeled and mashed

125 ml (4 fl oz/½ cup) rice malt syrup

2 teaspoons vanilla bean paste

2 egg whites

1 banana, extra, to serve

1 tablespoon honey, to glaze

Preheat the oven to 180°C (350°F). Grease or spray a 10 × 20 cm (4 × 8 inch) loaf tin with olive oil. Line the tin with baking paper.

In a large bowl, combine the self-raising flour, almond meal, protein powder, coconut and cinnamon. Add the mashed banana, rice malt syrup, vanilla bean paste and egg whites, and mix until just combined.

Spoon the mix into the loaf tin and top with the extra banana, halved lengthways. Bake for 45–50 minutes. If you see that the bread begins to brown too much on the top before it's cooked through, cover the loaf with foil for the remainder of the cooking time. Brush the top with honey while the loaf is still warm, then allow to cool.

MAKES 1 LOAF, AROUND 10 SLICES

tip Serve with vanilla cream: mix 300 ml (10½ fl oz) of thick (double) cream with 2 teaspoons of vanilla bean paste.

PANCAKES 3 WAYS

DF | GF | P | SF | V (LEAN)
1494 KJ/357 CAL PER SERVE

APPLE CINNAMON PANCAKES

3 tablespoons coconut oil

2 pink lady apples, peeled, cored and diced

1 teaspoon ground cinnamon

2 eggs (free-range, organic), whisked

2 bananas (very ripe, almost overripe is best), peeled and mashed

35 g (1¼ oz/¼ cup) self-raising flour (optional)

2 tablespoons almond spread

½ teaspoon ground nutmeg

1 teaspoon natural vanilla extract

1–2 tablespoons honey or rice malt syrup

Melt 1 tablespoon of coconut oil in a frying pan over medium heat. Add the apple and cinnamon, stirring to combine. Cook for 6 minutes or until the apple has softened.

To make the pancake batter, blend the eggs, banana, flour (if using), almond spread, nutmeg and vanilla extract together in a blender or food processor.

When cooked, remove half of the apple from the frying pan and set aside to cool slightly, before adding to the pancake mixture and combining well.

For the topping, add 1 tablespoon of the coconut oil and honey (or rice malt syrup, if using) to the remaining apple mixture, and stir to combine over the heat. When the oil has melted and all the ingredients are combined, remove from the heat.

Heat the remaining oil in a frying pan over low heat and spoon in 2 tablespoons of the batter. Cook until bubbles begin to form on the top. When it is golden underneath turn it over and cook for a few more minutes. Put the cooked pancakes on a serving platter and finish with the apple topping.

SERVES 4

GF | NF | SF | V (LEAN) (FAST)
460 KJ/110 CAL PER PANCAKE

LEAN CHOCOLATE PANCAKES

3 eggs (free-range, organic)

3 tablespoons unsweetened cocoa or cacao powder

stevia (optional, if you want it a little sweeter)

1 banana (very ripe, almost overripe is best), peeled and chopped

1 tablespoon coconut oil, melted

2 teaspoons butter, for frying

40 g (1½ oz/⅓ cup) raspberries, to serve

1 tablespoon shredded coconut, to serve

Add cocoa powder (or cacao, if using) and stevia to the eggs and whisk to combine.

In a blender, put the banana and the egg mixture and process to combine. Add coconut oil and process again to combine. Transfer from the blender to a bowl.

Heat a lightly greased frying pan over low heat. Put about 3 tablespoons of the batter into the pan, cooking for a few minutes or until bubbles begin to form on the top. Check the pancake is golden underneath before flipping it over and cooking for a further couple of minutes. Repeat with remaining batter.

Top with raspberries and shredded coconut to serve.

MAKES 6

DF | GF | NF | SF | V (LEAN) (FAST)
912 KJ/218 CAL PER SERVE

COCO-VANILLA PANCAKES

2 bananas (very ripe, almost overripe is best), peeled and chopped

3 eggs (free-range, organic)

2 tablespoons vanilla bean paste

50 g (1¾ oz/⅓ cup) coconut flour

½ teaspoon ground cinnamon

¼ teaspoon baking powder

125 ml (4 fl oz/½ cup) coconut or almond milk (carton variety)

1 tablespoon coconut oil

1 tablespoon rice malt syrup, to serve

4 fresh strawberries, to serve

Put the banana in a blender and process until smooth. Add the eggs and blend again quickly; you only want to just combine the eggs with the banana.

Add the vanilla bean paste to the blender, along with the coconut flour, cinnamon, baking powder and milk.

Blend until smooth.

Heat the coconut oil in a frying pan over low heat. Spoon 2–3 tablespoons of the pancake mix into the pan, cooking for a few minutes until bubbles begin to form on the top. Check the pancake is golden underneath before flipping it over and cooking for a further couple of minutes.

When all the pancakes are cooked, serve with a drizzle of rice malt syrup and top with the strawberries. Enjoy.

SERVES 4

FRIED EGGS WITH CHILLI RELISH

DAIRY-FREE | NUT-FREE | VEGETARIAN | 2640 KJ/631 CAL PER SERVE

3 tablespoons olive oil

1 long red chilli, halved, seeded and finely chopped

2 garlic cloves, minced

200 g (7 oz) sweet cherry tomatoes, halved

2 tablespoons soy sauce

½ teaspoon brown sugar (or ½ teaspoon stevia)

250 g (9 oz) white or brown rice, to serve

250 g (9 oz/1 small bunch) baby bok choy (pak choy), washed and sliced into ribbons

4 eggs (free-range, organic)

To make the chilli relish, heat 1 tablespoon of the olive oil in a frying pan over medium–high heat. Add the chilli and garlic and fry for 1–2 minutes or until softened and aromatic. Add the cherry tomatoes and stir until softened and the skin has browned and blistered. Add the soy sauce and brown sugar (or stevia) to the pan and cook for 5–8 minutes, stirring occasionally. Remove from the heat and transfer to a bowl.

Cook the rice according to your preferred method. Stir half the chilli relish into the rice and let it sit, to absorb the flavour.

Put another tablespoon of olive oil in the frying pan and add the bok choy, stirring for about 2 minutes or until wilted. Add the rice and relish mixture. Remove from the heat and transfer to a bowl.

Heat the remaining tablespoon of olive oil in the frying pan and break the eggs into the pan, cooking to your liking (we prefer sunny side up).

To serve, divide the rice and bok choy mixture between two breakfast bowls and top with the eggs. Serve with extra chilli relish on the side.

SERVES 2

YOU MET YOUR MATCHA YOGHURT BREKKIE BOWL

GLUTEN-FREE | SUGAR-FREE | VEGETARIAN | 2402 KJ/574 CAL PER SERVE

260 g (9¼ oz/1 cup) vanilla yoghurt (or your yoghurt of choice)

2 teaspoons matcha (available from health food shops)

½ red apple, cored and shredded

¼ cup chopped nuts of your choice (we love almonds, pistachios and cashews)

½ ruby red grapefruit, peeled, pith removed and sliced

1 tablespoon rice malt syrup

Put the yoghurt in a bowl, then sift the matcha into the yoghurt. Whisk well. Top with the apple, sprinkle with the nuts, then garnish with the grapefruit slices. Drizzle the rice malt syrup over the top.

SERVES 1

KALE & BEAN JUMBLE

DAIRY-FREE | GLUTEN-FREE | NUT-FREE | SUGAR-FREE | VEGETARIAN | VEGAN | 1527 KJ/365 CAL PER SERVE

2 tablespoons coconut oil (or olive oil)

1 desiree potato, diced into 5 mm–1 cm
(¼–³⁄₈ inch) cubes

pink salt and freshly ground black pepper

400 g (14 oz) tin cannellini beans,
drained and rinsed

1 brown onion, diced

100 g (3½ oz/4 cups) kale ribbons (stalks
removed, leaves sliced)

zest and juice of 1 lemon

45 g (1½ oz/½ cup) coarsely grated
parmesan cheese (optional)

Put the coconut oil in a large saucepan over medium–high heat, add the potato and season with salt and pepper. Cover with a lid and leave to brown for 5–8 minutes, stirring a few times during cooking. You want the potato to be browned on all sides.

Add the beans and the onion and mix well. Cook, stirring, for a few minutes or until the onion has softened. Add the kale ribbons and lemon juice and stir until the kale is wilted.

Remove from the heat and stir in the lemon zest and parmesan, if using. Taste and adjust seasoning if required. Serve immediately.

SERVES 2

tip   One bunch of kale equals 4 cups of kale ribbons.

CHIA PUDDINGS 4 WAYS

DF | GF | P | SF | VG
849 KJ/203 CAL PER SERVE

RASPBERRY CHIA PUDDING

250 g (9 oz/2 cups) fresh or frozen raspberries

250 ml (9 fl oz/1 cup) unsweetened almond milk

1 teaspoon stevia

2 tablespoons chia seeds

Put the raspberries into a small bowl, add the milk and then mash the berries gently. Add the stevia and stir. Add the chia seeds and stir again, making sure that all the ingredients are combined.

Pour into two Mason (preserving) jars or other glass containers and close the lids tightly. Refrigerate overnight.

These puddings will last in the fridge for 3 days.

SERVES 2

DF | GF | P | SF | VG
477 KJ/114 CAL PER SERVE

CHOCOLATE CHIA PUDDING

250 ml (9 fl oz/1 cup) unsweetened almond milk

2 teaspoons cocoa or cacao powder

1 tablespoon stevia

2 tablespoons chia seeds

Put all the ingredients in a small bowl and stir well to combine.

Pour into two Mason (preserving) jars or other glass containers and close the lids tightly. Refrigerate overnight.

These puddings will last in the fridge for 3 days.

SERVES 2

DF | GF | NF | P | SF | VG
1594 KJ/381 CAL PER SERVE

COCONUT CHIA PUDDING

500 ml (17 fl oz/2 cups) coconut milk (carton variety)

4 tablespoons shredded coconut

4 tablespoons chia seeds

2 teaspoons stevia

Put all the ingredients in a small bowl and stir well to combine. Cover and leave to set in the bowl overnight.

These puddings will last in the fridge for 3 days.

SERVES 2

tip To serve, scoop the pudding out of the bowl and layer in a Mason jar with chopped, fresh mango.

DF | GF | P | SF | VG
1414 KJ/338 CAL PER SERVE

ALMOND MAPLE CHIA PUDDING

500 ml (17 fl oz/2 cups) unsweetened almond milk

4 tablespoons chia seeds

2 teaspoons stevia

4 tablespoons maple syrup

Put all the ingredients in a small bowl and stir well to combine. Cover and leave to set in the bowl overnight.

These puddings will last in the fridge for 3 days.

SERVES 2

tip To serve, scoop the pudding out of the bowl and layer in a Mason jar with the chocolate chia pudding.

KEFALONIA CHEESE WITH LEMON & OREGANO

NUT-FREE | SUGAR-FREE | VEGETARIAN | 2410 KJ/576 CAL PER SERVE

225 g (8 oz/1½ cups) plain (all-purpose) flour

½ teaspoon baking powder

1 teaspoon salt

2 tablespoons rice malt syrup (or honey)

250 ml (9 fl oz/1 cup) cold soda water (plus a little more, if needed)

sea salt and ground black pepper

250 g (9 oz) goat's cheese (such as a chevre, not marinated or in liquid)

zest of ½ lemon

2 teaspoons very finely chopped oregano leaves

80 ml (2¾ fl oz/⅓ cup) rice bran oil, for frying

Start by making the batter: in a large mixing bowl, sift 150 g (5½ oz/1 cup) of flour with the baking powder and the salt and stir the ingredients together. Add the rice malt syrup (or honey, if using). Slowly add the soda water, whisking until the batter becomes smooth (no lumps). Put the batter in the fridge until it's time to fry the cheese.

In a small bowl, put the remaining 75 g (2½ oz/½ cup) of flour, a pinch of sea salt and ground black pepper. Use a fork to mix the ingredients together well, and set aside.

Line a tray with baking paper. Put the goat's cheese in a bowl with the lemon zest and oregano. Mix well and use your hands to roll the mixture into 12 small, evenly sized balls (you don't want them to be too big). Place each ball onto the baking paper and then put the tray in the fridge for about 45 minutes.

Heat the oil in a heavy-based saucepan or a deep-fryer over a high heat. Line a plate or tray with paper towel and put to the side.

Remove the goat's cheese balls and the batter from the fridge. Roll a cheese ball first in the dry seasoned flour mixture, then dip into the batter, making sure that the cheese is fully coated in the batter. Drop them VERY carefully, a few at a time, into the pan of oil and use a slotted spoon to keep them from sticking to each other. When they turn a golden brown colour, use the slotted spoon to transfer them to the plate with the paper towel (to absorb excess oil).

Once you've finished frying all of the cheese balls, transfer them to a serving platter. Serve immediately.

SERVES 4

FAB BREKKIE COUSCOUS

DAIRY-FREE | SUGAR-FREE | VEGAN | 2238 KJ/535 CAL PER SERVE

zest of 1 orange

juice of 4 oranges

½ teaspoon ground cinnamon

1 teaspoon orange flower water (or
½ teaspoon orange extract)

1 tablespoon coconut oil

2 tablespoons rice malt syrup, plus
1 tablespoon extra to serve

190 g (6¾ oz/1 cup) couscous

6 fresh dates, pitted and chopped

45 g (1½ oz/¼ cup) dried apricots,
chopped

55 g (2 oz/⅓ cup) dried cranberries

small handful of mint leaves, torn

2 tablespoons pepitas (pumpkin seeds),
to serve

2 tablespoons chopped pistachio nuts,
to serve

4 teaspoons pomegranate molasses,
to serve

Combine the orange zest and juice in a medium saucepan and bring to the boil. Remove from the heat and stir in the cinnamon, orange flower water (or orange extract, if using), coconut oil and rice malt syrup.

Put the couscous in a large heatproof bowl, and pour the still hot orange mixture over the top. Cover, then fluff the couscous with a fork. Stir the chopped dates, apricots and half the cranberries and mint into the couscous.

Spoon the couscous mixture into four bowls, and sprinkle with the pepitas, the remaining cranberries and mint and the chopped pistachios. Drizzle with rice malt syrup and pomegranate molasses and serve immediately.

SERVES 4

SMOOTHIE BOWLS 3 WAYS

DF | GF | P | SF | VG
1167 KJ/279 CAL PER SERVE

THE ABC SMOOTHIE BOWL

250 ml (9 fl oz/1 cup) unsweetened almond milk

2 tablespoons almond (or other nut) spread

2 peeled bananas, 1 fresh and 1 frozen

2 tablespoons unsweetened cocoa or cacao powder

45 g (1½ oz/1 cup) baby spinach leaves

2 Medjool dates, pitted and roughly chopped

stevia, to taste

shredded coconut (optional), to serve

raspberries (optional), to serve

Place the milk, almond spread, frozen banana, cocoa, spinach, dates and stevia in a blender and process until smooth. Pour into a bowl.

Slice the fresh banana and arrange on top of the smoothie. Sprinkle the shredded coconut and raspberries on top of the bowl, if using. Serve and enjoy.

SERVES 2

DF | GF | P | SF | VG
1125 KJ/269 CAL PER SERVE

SUPERFOOD SMOOTHIE BOWL

250 ml (9 fl oz/1 cup) unsweetened almond milk

90 g (3¼ oz/2 cups) baby spinach leaves

7 g (¼ oz/¼ cup) kale ribbons (stalks removed, leaves sliced)

1 large frozen peeled banana

¼ small avocado, peeled, stone removed

1 tablespoon coconut oil, melted

3 teaspoons liquid chlorophyll (spearmint flavour is fine)

1 teaspoon chia seeds

stevia, to taste

2 tablespoons mixed berries, to serve

1 tablespoon mixed nuts, to serve

Put the milk, spinach, kale, banana, avocado, coconut oil, chlorophyll, chia seeds and stevia in a blender, and blend until smooth. Pour into a bowl, and top with the mixed berries and mixed nuts.

SERVES 2

DF | GF | NF | P | SF | VG
1188 KJ/284 CAL PER SERVE

ACAI BREKKIE BOWL

250 ml (9 fl oz/1 cup) coconut milk (we use the carton variety, which is a blend of coconut and almond or rice milk)

1 frozen peeled banana

1 tablespoon acai powder

1 tablespoon coconut oil, melted

70 g (2½ oz/½ cup) frozen mixed berries

1 kiwi fruit, cut into thick slices

1 passionfruit, scooped out of skin

Put the milk, banana, acai, coconut oil and frozen berries into a blender and process until smooth.

Pour the smoothie into a bowl and top with kiwi fruit and passionfruit. Serve immediately and enjoy.

SERVES 2

tip If you don't have a commercial quality blender, blend the liquid and leafy greens first, before slowly adding other ingredients. You can also chop your ingredients into smaller pieces before adding them to the blender.

SPICY SMASHED AVOCADO & EGGS

NUT-FREE | SUGAR-FREE | VEGETARIAN | 3163 KJ/756 CAL PER SERVE

4 slices sourdough bread, for toasting

8 vine-ripened cherry tomatoes, halved

1 tablespoon olive oil

1 avocado, peeled, stone removed

2 tablespoons harissa paste, more if you would like it very spicy (see our recipe on page 218, or use purchased harissa)

100 g (3½ oz) feta cheese, crumbled

4 eggs (free-range, organic)

zest of 1 small lemon

Turn on a griller (broiler) to a high heat setting. Line a baking tray with baking paper and lay the slices of sourdough on top. Toast both sides of the sourdough lightly. They will go back under the griller again, so a light toasting should do. You can also simply do this step in a toaster, if you prefer. Remove the tray once the sourdough has toasted, and set aside.

Wash the cherry tomatoes and make a small slit in each one, being careful not to dislodge them from the vine. Heat the oil in a frying pan over a high heat. Add the tomatoes and cook until the skin blisters and they begin to caramelise slightly.

Put the avocado in a small bowl and sprinkle with a little salt and pepper (to taste). Smash the avocado lightly with a fork.

Spread the harissa paste evenly across all of the sourdough slices (half a tablespoon for each slice or to taste).

Next, divide the avocado equally and spread it onto the sourdough slices. Top with feta and set aside.

Poach the eggs or cook them your favourite way (scrambled for Sally, soft-boiled for Maha!). A couple of minutes before the eggs have finished cooking, return the baking tray with the toast to the griller. Keep an eye on the toast to make sure that it doesn't burn: the aim is for the cheese to melt on top of the avocado.

Top each piece of toast with a cooked egg. Sprinkle a little lemon zest over the top and serve with a side of cherry tomatoes.

SERVES 2

tip Harissa paste is available from gourmet food shops or grocers.

RED VELVET PANCAKES

NF | SF | V | 1: 2305 KJ/551 CAL PER SERVE | 2: 2184 KJ/522 CAL PER SERVE | 3: 2481 KJ/593 CAL PER SERVE

2 large eggs (free-range, organic)

1 vanilla bean, split and seeds scraped

3 tablespoons rice malt syrup (or honey)

225 g (8 oz/1½ cups) plain (all-purpose) flour (or coconut flour)

5 tablespoons sugar, or stevia

1 teaspoon baking powder

2 small cooked beetroot (beets) (available in vacuum-sealed packs), chopped

375 ml (13½ fl oz/1½ cups) skim milk (or oat milk)

1 tablespoon butter, for frying

Option 1: Coconut topping

2 x 270 ml (9½ fl oz) tin Ayam coconut milk, refrigerated overnight

2 tablespoons rice malt syrup (optional)

300 g (11 oz/2 punnets) mixed berries

2 tablespoons shredded coconut

Option 2: Vanilla cream

85 g (3 oz/⅓ cup) cream cheese

1 vanilla bean, split and seeds scraped

2 tablespoons Greek-style yoghurt

Option 3: Chocolate

2 tablespoons unsweetened cocoa powder

4 tablespoons rice malt syrup

2 tablespoons coconut oil

fresh berries (optional), to serve

Start by making the pancakes. Whisk together the eggs, vanilla seeds and rice malt syrup. Set aside. Sift the flour, sugar (or stevia, if using) and baking powder into a large mixing bowl.

Using a blender or food processor, blend the beetroot with the milk until you have a smooth consistency. Add to the egg mixture and stir together until totally combined and smooth. Add the egg and beetroot mixture to the flour. Whisk until smooth.

Melt a knob of butter in a frying pan over low heat. Put about 3 tablespoons of batter into the pan, cooking for a few minutes or until bubbles begin to form on the top. Check the pancake is firm underneath before flipping over and cooking for a further couple of minutes. Repeat with the remainder of the batter.

When cooked, transfer the pancakes to a serving platter. Choose which topping you want to have. Makes 12 pancakes.

To make the coconut topping, take the tins of coconut milk out of the fridge and remove the hardened cream (about 135 ml/ 4½ fl oz), putting it into a bowl. Stir the cream until it softens. Serve the pancakes, drizzled with the rice malt syrup (optional) and topped with the cream, berries and shredded coconut.

To make the vanilla cream topping, mix together all of the ingredients until well combined and smooth. Serve on top of the pancakes.

For the chocolate topping, whisk together all of the ingredients until well combined and smooth. To make the sauce runny, zap it in the microwave for 10–15 seconds. Drizzle on top of the pancakes when serving and top with the berries (if using).

SERVES 4

the GOOD life

EASY OVERNIGHT OATS

DAIRY-FREE | NUT-FREE | SUGAR-FREE | VEGETARIAN | VEGAN | 1184 KJ/283 CAL PER SERVE

190 g (6¾ oz/2 cups) rolled oats

500 ml (17 fl oz/2 cups) coconut milk
(carton variety)

1 tablespoon shredded coconut, plus
1 tablespoon extra to serve

½ teaspoon vanilla bean paste (or
natural vanilla extract)

zest and juice of 1 small orange, plus
extra zest to serve

1 tablespoon honey or rice malt syrup,
to taste

In a large bowl, combine oats, coconut milk, shredded coconut, vanilla bean paste (or extract, if using) together with the zest and juice of the orange. Mix the ingredients together well, and stand in the fridge overnight.

Remove from the fridge and serve at room temperature, or heat in the microwave for 45–60 seconds.

Drizzle with honey or rice malt syrup, to taste. Top with extra shredded coconut and extra orange zest.

SERVES 4

tip Make a larger batch, cover and store in the fridge for up to 2 days.

RUSTIC TOMATO & SPINACH SCRAMBLED EGGS

DAIRY-FREE | GLUTEN-FREE | NUT-FREE | PALEO | SUGAR-FREE | VEGETARIAN | 1418 KJ/339 CAL PER SERVE

250 g (9 oz/1 punnet) sweet cherry tomatoes

2 tablespoons olive oil

1 garlic clove, finely chopped

2 spring onions (scallions), finely chopped

180 g (6¼ oz/4 cups) baby spinach leaves

dried chilli flakes, to taste

4 eggs (free-range, organic)

sourdough toast, to serve (optional)

Wash the cherry tomatoes and make a small cut in each one with a sharp knife. Set aside.

Put 1 tablespoon of the olive oil into a heavy-based frying pan and heat over medium–high heat. Add the garlic and cherry tomatoes, stirring, for about 4–5 minutes or until the tomatoes begin to blister and caramelise slightly.

Transfer the tomato mixture to a bowl and leave the pan on the heat. Add the remaining olive oil. Once heated, add the spring onions, baby spinach and a small pinch of chilli flakes (to taste). Stir very gently until the spinach has wilted.

Return the tomato mixture to the pan with the spinach, mix to combine and transfer to a bowl.

Crack the eggs into a separate bowl and use a fork to break the yolks and whisk lightly. Pour the eggs into the pan. Using a wooden spoon or spatula, gently stir the eggs until they have just cooked through. Fold the tomato mixture through the eggs.

Serve immediately, with toasted sourdough (if using).

SERVES 2

MUM'S LABNEH 3 WAYS

GLUTEN-FREE | NUT-FREE | SUGAR-FREE | VEGETARIAN | 653 KJ/156 CAL PER BALL, DRAINED

1 kg (2 lb 4 oz) tub of Greek-style yoghurt

1 litre (35 fl oz/4 cups) olive oil

dried chilli flakes (optional)

fresh oregano (optional)

zest of 1 lemon (optional)

Special equipment

Large square of muslin (cheesecloth) about the size of a tea towel (dish towel)

Use the muslin to line a large sieve and place the sieve over a large, deep bowl. Pour the yoghurt into the muslin and tie the corners of the cloth together very tightly (as though you were tying a sack). Transfer to the fridge and leave to drain for 48–72 hours. Squeeze any excess whey (liquid) out of the cheesecloth and then discard the liquid from the bowl. You'll be left with the labneh.

Make labneh balls by taking a heaped tablespoon of labneh and rolling it into a ball between your hands. Put the balls into a glass jar, cover with olive oil and refrigerate with the lid on.

There are so many ways to enjoy labneh: serve plain with a sprinkle of salt on top of olive sourdough toast; drizzle with za'atar and spread onto pitta bread for a snack; eat as a dip with carrot and celery sticks.

For two other ways you can add flavour to your labneh, infuse the olive oil in the jar:

- add a teaspoon of dried chilli flakes to the olive oil (more if you want it super spicy!)

- add a sprig of fresh oregano and the zest of 1 lemon to the olive oil

Labneh should last in the fridge for several weeks.

MAKES 16 LABNEH BALLS

LABNEH & FIG TARTINE

SUGAR-FREE | VEGETARIAN | 1791 KJ/428 CAL PER SERVE

4 x 50 g (1¾ oz) labneh balls (plain)

2 figs, washed, stems removed

2 tablespoons shelled pistachio nuts

4 slices sourdough bread

2 tablespoons honey (for drizzling)

Remove labneh balls from the fridge and bring to room temperature.

Meanwhile, slice the figs into 5 mm (¼ inch) thick slices. Roughly chop the pistachios.

Toast the sourdough and set aside. Once it has cooled slightly, spread the labneh evenly onto the sourdough slices and lay the fig slices on top. Drizzle the honey across the figs and top with the pistachios.

Serve immediately.

SERVES 2

SKILLET BAKED EGGS

DAIRY-FREE | GLUTEN-FREE | NUT-FREE | PALEO | SUGAR-FREE | VEGETARIAN | 1418 KJ/339 CAL PER SERVE

2 tablespoons olive oil

½ garlic clove, minced

½ leek (white part only), thinly sliced

200 g (7 oz/4½ cups) baby spinach leaves

juice of ½ lemon

1 long red chilli, seeded and chopped

4 eggs (free-range, organic)

40 g (1½ oz) fried pancetta, chopped, to serve (optional)

Preheat the oven to 150°C (300°F).

Heat the olive oil in a frying pan over medium heat. Add the garlic and leek and cook, stirring frequently until soft. Add the spinach, lemon juice and half of the chilli, then season with salt and pepper to taste. Cook for a few minutes, stirring frequently, until the spinach has wilted.

Drain any liquid from the spinach mixture and transfer it to an ovenproof skillet or shallow baking dish. Make four indentations in the spinach mixture. Crack an egg into a cup, then carefully pour it into one of the indentations, taking care not to break the yolk. Repeat with the remaining eggs.

Bake the eggs for 10–12 minutes or until the egg whites are set.

Serve immediately, topped with pancetta and the remaining chilli.

SERVES 2

Tips
- Put a teaspoon of full-fat ricotta cheese in the bottom of each indentation, before adding the egg.
- Quarter a handful of sweet cherry tomatoes and add them to the pan to cook with the spinach.

ZUCCHINI, FETA & MINT FRITTERS

NUT-FREE | SUGAR-FREE | VEGETARIAN | 1079 KJ/258 CAL PER SERVE

3 zucchini (courgettes), coarsely grated

½ brown onion, finely sliced

2 small eggs (free-range, organic)

65 g (2¼ oz/½ cup) feta cheese, crumbled

1 tablespoon finely chopped mint leaves

55 g (2 oz/½ cup) dried breadcrumbs

2 tablespoons olive oil

80 ml (2¾ fl oz/⅓ cup) Greek-style yoghurt, to serve

handful of mint leaves, roughly chopped, to serve

Put the grated zucchini into a sieve and allow liquid to drain for about an hour. Squeeze as much liquid out of the zucchini as possible and pat dry with paper towel.

Transfer the zucchini to a bowl, together with the onion, eggs, feta, mint and breadcrumbs. Mix to combine well and season with salt and pepper.

Heat the oil in a nonstick frying pan over medium–high heat. Take a large, heaped tablespoon of the zucchini mixture and spread it out in the pan. Cook through, ensuring that the fritter is browned on both sides. Repeat with the remainder of the zucchini mixture.

Once each fritter has been cooked, transfer it to a plate covered with a couple of thicknesses of paper towel (to absorb any excess oil).

Put the yoghurt in a small bowl. Season with a little salt and top with mint leaves.

Serve the fritters with the mint yoghurt.

SERVES 4

YOGHURT BRÛLÉE

NUT-FREE | VEGETARIAN | 1556 KJ/372 CAL PER SERVE

140 g (5 oz/1 cup) mixed fresh raspberries and blueberries, plus extra to serve

1 tablespoon maple syrup

1 kg (2 lb 4 oz) tub of Greek-style yoghurt (not low-fat)

75 g (2½ oz/⅓ cup lightly packed) brown sugar

Special equipment

brûlée torch

Put a layer of berries in the bottom of each of four small ramekins or breakfast bowls. Drizzle a teaspoon of maple syrup over the berries in each of the ramekins. Next fill the ramekins with the yoghurt and ensure the top of the yoghurt is smooth (you can use the back of a spoon to help achieve this).

Evenly sprinkle 1 tablespoon of brown sugar over the top of each ramekin of yoghurt, and use the brûlée torch to create a crisp cover.

Serve immediately with the extra berries.

SERVES 4

BABY BOK CHOY FRITTATA

GLUTEN-FREE | NUT-FREE | SUGAR-FREE | VEGETARIAN | 1155 KJ/276 CAL PER SERVE

8 large eggs (free-range, organic)

1 tablespoon olive oil

1 small red (Spanish) onion, sliced

1.2 kg (2 lb 12 oz/3 bunches) baby bok choy (pak choy), washed and sliced into ribbons

50 g (1¾ oz) chargrilled red capsicum (pepper) strips (available from the supermarket or delis), drained of oil and sliced

50 g (1¾ oz/⅓ cup) feta cheese, crumbled

Preheat a griller (broiler) on medium–high to 200°C (400°F).

Crack the eggs into a bowl and whisk together. Season with salt and pepper and set aside.

Heat the olive oil in an ovenproof pan over medium heat on the stovetop. Add the onion and cook for about 2 minutes or until softened. Add the bok choy and stir until wilted and cooked through.

Reduce the heat slightly and add the eggs. Stir into the onion. Add the red capsicum strips and goat's cheese, distributing them evenly across the pan. Cook for 8–10 minutes.

Remove the pan from the stovetop and transfer it to the griller (broiler) for 8–10 minutes or until set. Serve immediately.

SERVES 4–6

tip Store leftovers in an airtight container in the fridge for up to 2 days.

super green

cherry
on top

energy
elixir

lean life

choc
berry fix

pine
lime

smoothies

cauli
crush

mega green
skinny

green 'n'
lean

antioxidant
booster

coco loco

SUPER GREEN SMOOTHIES

(LEAN) (FAST)

DF | GF | P | SF | VG
1293 KJ/309 CAL PER SERVE

ENERGY ELIXIR

375 ml (13 fl oz/1½ cups) unsweetened almond milk

45 g (1½ oz/1 cup) baby spinach leaves

12 g (½ oz/½ cup) kale ribbons (stalks removed, leaves sliced)

1 tablespoon chia seeds

1 frozen peeled banana

1 kiwi fruit

stevia, to taste

SERVES 1

(LEAN) (FAST)

GF | NF | SF | V
1297 KJ/310 CAL PER SERVE

CHERRY ON TOP

90 g (3¼ oz/2 cups) baby spinach leaves

150 g (5½ oz/1 cup) cherries, pitted

70 g (2½ oz/½ cup) mixed berries

1 frozen peeled banana

250 ml (9 fl oz/1 cup) skim milk

SERVES 1

(FAB) (FAST)

GF | NF | SF | V
2000 KJ/478 CAL PER SERVE

COCO LOCO

250 ml (9 fl oz/1 cup) coconut milk (carton variety)

20 g (¾ oz/¼ cup) shredded coconut

1 teaspoon coconut oil

130 g (4½ oz/½ cup) Greek-style yoghurt

45 g (1½ oz/1 cup) baby spinach leaves

30 g (1 oz/½ cup) broccoli florets

½ lime, peeled and seeded

½ teaspoon stevia

ice cubes, to achieve desired consistency

SERVES 1

(LEAN) (FAST)

GF | NF | SF | V
1644 KJ/393 CAL PER SERVE

CAULI CRUSH

250 ml (9 fl oz/1 cup) skim or full-fat milk

130 g (4½ oz/½ cup) vanilla yoghurt

90 g (3¼ oz/¾ cup) cauliflower florets

¼ avocado, peeled, stone removed

300 g (10½ oz/2 cups) strawberries, hulled

2 teaspoons natural vanilla extract

stevia, to taste

SERVES 1

(LEAN) (FAST)

DF | GF | NF | SF | VG
301 KJ/72 CAL PER SERVE

LEAN LIFE

25 g (1 oz/1 cup) kale ribbons (stalks removed, leaves sliced)

45 g (1½ oz/1 cup) baby spinach leaves

½ Lebanese (short) cucumber

1 cm (3/8 inch) piece of ginger

a few parsley leaves

1 lemon, peeled and seeded

1 lime (skin on)

250 ml (9 fl oz/1 cup) water

handful of ice cubes

SERVES 1

(LEAN) (FAST)

DF | GF | P | SF | VG
1360 KJ/325 CAL PER SERVE

ANTIOXIDANT BOOSTER

375 ml (13 fl oz/1½ cups) unsweetened almond milk

65 g (2¼ oz/1½ cups) baby spinach leaves

1 frozen peeled banana

1 tablespoon unsweetened cocoa powder

1 tablespoon chia seeds

½ teaspoon natural vanilla extract

stevia, to taste

SERVES 1

the GOOD *life*

SUPER GREEN SMOOTHIES

(LEAN) (FAST)

DF | GF | NF | P | SF | VG
703 KJ/168 CAL PER SERVE

PINE LIME

250 ml (9 fl oz/1 cup) coconut water

60 ml (2 fl oz/¼ cup) coconut milk
(carton variety)

65 g (2¼ oz/1½ cups) baby spinach leaves

½ small Lebanese (short) cucumber

120 g (4¼ oz/¾ cup) chopped pineapple

¼ frozen lime, skin on (more for zing)

SERVES 1

(LEAN) (FAST)

DF | GF | NF | P | SF | VG
1008 KJ/241 CAL PER SERVE

MEGA GREEN SKINNY

250 ml (9 fl oz/1 cup) coconut water

90 g (3¼ oz/2 cups) baby spinach leaves

12 g (½ oz/½ cup) kale ribbons (stalks
removed, leaves sliced)

1 ruby red grapefruit, peeled

1 frozen banana, peeled

SERVES 1

(LEAN) (FAST)

DF | GF | NF | P | SF | VG
628 KJ/150 CAL PER SERVE

GREEN 'N' LEAN

250 ml (9 fl oz/1 cup) coconut water

90 g (3¼ oz/2 cups) baby spinach leaves

15 g (½ oz/¼ cup) broccoli florets

½ frozen peeled banana

80 g (3 oz/1 cup) chopped honeydew melon

½ cup ice cubes

SERVES 1

(LEAN) (FAST)

GF | NF | P | SF | V
1213 KJ/290 CAL PER SERVE

CHOC BERRY FIX

250 ml (9 fl oz/1 cup) skim milk

90 g (3¼ oz/2 cups) baby spinach leaves

1 frozen peeled banana

60 g (2 oz/½ cup) frozen raspberries

1 tablespoon unsweetened cocoa powder

5 g (¼ oz/¼ cup) mint leaves

½ teaspoon stevia

SERVES 1

Tips

- For each smoothie, put all the ingredients into a blender and blend until smooth. Enjoy!
- If you don't have a commercial-quality blender, blend the liquids and leafy greens first, before slowly adding other ingredients. You can also chop your ingredients into smaller pieces before adding them to the mixture.
- Choose the carton variety of coconut milk, which is typically coconut blended with rice milk and therefore lower in fat and kilojoules (calories).

lunch

LIME & BASIL PRAWNS

DAIRY-FREE | GLUTEN-FREE | NUT-FREE | PALEO | SUGAR-FREE | 1853 KJ/443 CAL PER SERVE

12 raw prawns (shrimp), peeled and deveined, tails left intact

1 teaspoon lime juice, plus extra for cooking

2 kaffir lime leaves, finely sliced

1½ teaspoons tom yum paste

1 garlic clove, minced

1 tablespoon olive oil

handful of basil leaves, finely sliced

3 tablespoons vegetable oil

lime wedges, to serve

In a large bowl, combine the prawns with the lime juice, kaffir lime leaves, tom yum paste, garlic, olive oil and basil. Mix well, ensuring that the prawns are well coated. Cover and set aside for 20 minutes.

Heat a barbecue or chargrill and brush with vegetable oil. Toss the prawns in the marinade again before placing them on the grill. Cook for a few minutes, turning over halfway through cooking. Remove from the heat as soon as the prawns turn pink and serve with lime wedges.

SERVES 2

TOMATO & RICOTTA CRUSTLESS TORTE

GLUTEN-FREE | NUT-FREE | SUGAR-FREE | VEGETARIAN | 1264 KJ/302 CAL PER SERVE

1 tablespoon olive oil

500 g (1 lb 2 oz) fresh ricotta (not low-fat)

150 g (5½ oz) Danish feta cheese, crumbled

45 g (1½ oz/½ cup) grated parmesan cheese

3 eggs (free-range, organic)

3 garlic cloves, crushed

small handful of basil leaves, finely sliced, plus extra to serve

400 g (14 oz) cherry tomato medley, halved (if you can't find a medley of tomatoes, then just use a mixture of red cherry tomatoes and golden cherry or grape tomatoes)

2 heirloom tomatoes, cut into thick slices

2 kumatoes, cut into thick slices

100 g (3½ oz) mixed salad leaves, to serve

Preheat the oven to 180°C (350°F). Lightly grease a 20 cm (8 inch) pie dish with the olive oil.

In a large bowl, using a whisk or an electric handmixer, combine the ricotta, feta, parmesan, eggs, garlic and sliced basil. Season with a pinch of salt and plenty of freshly ground black pepper.

Spoon the ricotta mixture into the pie dish. Arrange the red and yellow tomatoes, cut side up, with the heirloom tomato and kumato slices on top of the ricotta mixture.

Bake for 60 minutes or until set and golden. Remove from the oven and set aside to cool. Once cooled, transfer to the fridge for around 30 minutes just to firm up.

Top the torte with extra basil leaves. Serve with mixed salad leaves.

SERVES 6

CRISPY COCONUT CHICKEN & MANGO SALSA

DAIRY-FREE | NUT-FREE | SUGAR-FREE | 2025 KJ/484 CAL PER SERVE

500 g (1 lb 2 oz) boneless, skinless chicken breast, cut into 2.5 cm (1 inch) wide strips

35 g (1¼ oz/¼ cup) plain (all-purpose) flour

½ teaspoon salt

50 g (1¾ oz/1 cup) moist coconut flakes

60 g (2¼ oz/1 cup) panko (Japanese) breadcrumbs, seasoned to taste with salt and pepper

2 large eggs (free-range, organic)

2 tablespoons rice bran oil, for frying

Mango salsa

2 ripe mangoes, peeled and diced

1 red capsicum (pepper), diced

80 g (2¾ oz/½ cup) finely chopped red (Spanish) onion

15 g (½ oz/¼ cup) finely chopped coriander (cilantro) leaves

1 jalapeño pepper, finely diced (optional)

juice of 1 lime lime

To make the mango salsa, combine the mango, capsicum, red onion, coriander and jalapeño (if using) in a serving bowl. Drizzle with the lime juice and toss well. Season to taste with salt. For the best flavour, allow the mango salsa to rest for at least 10 minutes.

Lay the chicken strips between two sheets of baking paper and use a rolling pin or a meat mallet to flatten them into strips of even thickness.

Combine the flour and salt with some freshly ground black pepper in a shallow bowl large enough for the chicken pieces. In another bowl, combine the coconut and breadcrumbs. Break the eggs into a third bowl and beat with a fork.

Coat each strip of chicken in the flour first, then the egg and finally the coconut mixture.

Heat a large deep frying pan over medium–high heat. Add 1 tablespoon of rice bran oil to the pan and heat. Add about half the chicken strips to the pan and cook for about 2 minutes on each side or until cooked through and golden. Repeat with remaining chicken.

Serve with the mango salsa.

SERVES 4

WATERCRESS SOUP

DAIRY-FREE | GLUTEN-FREE | NUT-FREE | SUGAR-FREE | VEGETARIAN | 623 KJ/149 CAL PER SERVE

2 teaspoons butter, for cooking

1 large brown onion, peeled and chopped

1 garlic clove, finely chopped

1 potato, peeled and diced into 2 cm
(¾ inch) cubes

1 litre (35 fl oz/4 cups) chicken or
vegetable stock

200 g (7 oz/1 ⅓ cups) frozen peas

150 g (5½ oz) watercress (reserve a small
handful of leaves, to serve)

45 g (1½ oz/1 cup) baby spinach leaves

small handful of mint leaves, plus extra
to serve

1 tablespoon light sour cream (optional),
to serve

1 tablespoon olive oil, to serve

Melt a small knob of butter in a saucepan over medium heat and cook the onion and garlic, stirring until softened. Add the potato and cook for a couple of minutes. Add the stock and simmer for about 5 minutes. Add the peas, watercress and baby spinach leaves, and simmer for a further 3–5 minutes.

Remove from the heat, add the mint leaves and use a stick blender to process until smooth. Alternatively, carefully transfer in batches to an upright blender and blend until smooth. Taste and season with salt and pepper.

Serve immediately with a small dollop of sour cream (if using) and drizzle with olive oil. Garnish with the reserved watercress leaves and extra mint leaves.

SERVES 4

CHIA-SEARED TUNA WITH RAINBOW SALAD

GLUTEN-FREE | NUT-FREE | 1628 KJ/389 CAL PER SERVE

2 tablespoons sesame seeds

2 tablespoons black and white chia seeds

4 pieces tuna loin, approximately 100 g (3½ oz) each

1 tablespoon olive oil

Rainbow salad

2 carrots, peeled and julienned

1 parsnip, peeled and thinly sliced

1 green capsicum (pepper), thinly sliced

1 red capsicum (pepper), thinly sliced

1 small red (Spanish) onion, thinly sliced

2 tablespoons coriander (cilantro) leaves, finely chopped

Dressing

1 tablespoon sugar, or 1 teaspoon stevia

125 g (4½ oz/½ cup) light sour cream

2 tablespoons rice wine vinegar

To make the salad, combine the dressing ingredients in a bowl and season with salt and white pepper; add the vegetables and coriander. Mix gently. Allow to stand for 30 minutes while you prepare the tuna.

Combine the sesame seeds and chia seeds in a bowl and season with salt and pepper. Press the tuna steaks firmly into the bowl to ensure they are well coated with seeds.

Heat the olive oil in a large nonstick frying pan. Sear the tuna until lightly browned, about 2 minutes each side. Allow the tuna to rest for 3–4 minutes, then slice into 2 cm (¾ inch) strips.

Divide the rainbow salad among 4 plates and top with the tuna strips.

SERVES 4

zucchini

noodles 2 ways

ZUCCHINI NOODLES WITH AVOCADO PESTO

DAIRY-FREE | GLUTEN-FREE | PALEO | SUGAR-FREE | 2431 KJ/581 CAL PER SERVE

3 medium zucchini (courgettes)

30 g (1 oz/1 cup) basil leaves

1 avocado, peeled, stone removed, roughly chopped

juice of 1 small lemon

1 garlic clove, crushed

2 tablespoons pine nuts, toasted (or you can use cashews or walnuts)

60 ml (2 fl oz/¼ cup) olive oil

20 g (¾ oz/⅓ cup) shelled edamame beans, to serve

Use a spiraliser or peeler to make zucchini 'noodles'.

Put the basil, avocado, lemon juice, garlic and pine nuts into the bowl of a food processor and season with salt and pepper. Pulse, adding the olive oil a little at a time, until you achieve a pastelike texture. Taste and adjust seasoning if required.

Mix the zucchini noodles with the pesto, turning well until the zucchini noodles are coated.

Divide the noodles between two bowls and top each bowl with 2 tablespoons of edamame. Serve and enjoy.

SERVES 2

ZUCCHINI NOODLES WITH TOMATO & FETA

GLUTEN-FREE | NUT-FREE | SUGAR-FREE | VEGETARIAN | 653 KJ/156 CAL PER SERVE

3 medium zucchini (courgettes)

1 tablespoon olive oil

2 garlic cloves, crushed

400 g (14 oz) cherry tomato medley, halved (if you can't find a medley of tomatoes, then just use a mixture of red cherry tomatoes and golden cherry or grape tomatoes)

65 g (2½ oz/½ cup) crumbled Danish feta or goat's cheese

Use a spiraliser or peeler to make zucchini 'noodles'.

Heat the olive oil in a frying pan over medium heat. Add the garlic and stir until fragrant. Add half of the cherry tomatoes, half of the feta and the zucchini noodles, with a small pinch of salt and freshly ground black pepper to taste.

Mix well. Once the tomatoes have softened and slightly caramelised (about 4 minutes), transfer the noodle mix to a serving platter. Top with the remaining tomatoes and scatter the remaining feta over.

SERVES 2

SALMON CARPACCIO

DAIRY-FREE | GLUTEN-FREE | NUT-FREE | PALEO | SUGAR-FREE | 2075 KJ/496 CAL PER SERVE

300 g (10½ oz) sashimi-grade salmon

few pinches of sea salt, to taste

2 tablespoons extra virgin olive oil

2 tablespoons lemon juice

2 spring onions (scallions), finely chopped

3 teaspoons finely chopped dill

45 g (1½ oz/¼ cup) baby capers (jar variety in vinegar, rinsed and drained)

microherbs, to serve

toasted bread, to serve (optional)

With a long sharp knife, cut paper-thin slices of the salmon; start from the tail and work your way up.

Arrange the slices on a plate, sprinkle with sea salt, drizzle with the olive oil and lemon juice, then scatter with spring onion, dill, microherbs and capers.

Before serving, add some freshly ground pepper.

You can serve it immediately or cover it and leave it in the fridge until you are ready to serve with toasted bread.

SERVES 2

PULLED LAMB & SLAW TORTILLAS

NUT-FREE | SUGAR-FREE | 3427 KJ/819 CAL PER SERVE

1 lamb leg, on the bone (approximately 1.1 kg or 2 lb 7 oz)

8 sage leaves, chopped

3 tablespoons fresh thyme leaves

3 garlic cloves, minced

3–4 tablespoons extra virgin olive oil

12 mini tortillas

Slaw

1 pear, thinly sliced

80 g (2¾ oz/1 bunch) mint leaves, finely sliced

1 carrot, peeled and cut into thin batons

50 g (1¾ oz/2 cups) kale ribbons (stalks removed, leaves sliced)

¼ red cabbage, finely shredded

1 tablespoon extra virgin olive oil

80 ml (2½ fl oz/⅓ cup) apple cider vinegar

Yoghurt dressing

250 g (9 oz) Greek-style yoghurt

juice of ¼ lime

zest of ½ lime

Trim the lamb leg of excess fat and put it in a roasting pan.

Combine the sage, thyme, garlic and olive oil in a small bowl and season with salt and pepper. Toss to combine well. Spread the marinade over the lamb leg and leave to marinate for 30 minutes at room temperature, or preferably in the fridge overnight. Ensure the lamb comes to room temperature for 15–20 minutes before cooking. This allows it to cook evenly.

Preheat the oven to 160°C (315°F). Add 125 ml (4 fl oz/½ cup) of water to the roasting dish with the lamb and cover tightly with foil. Cook the lamb for 3 hours or until tender enough to shred with two forks. Shred the lamb, discarding any fat, and season to taste.

Meanwhile, combine all of the ingredients for the slaw and toss gently.

Combine the yoghurt, lime juice and zest for the dressing.

Fill the tortillas with slaw, top with the shredded lamb and a dollop of yoghurt dressing.

SERVES 4

TIP The lamb can be cooked and shredded in advance and simply reheated when you're ready to serve. If you have the time, leave the lamb in the oven for an extra 30 minutes to 1 hour. It gets tastier and falls apart even more easily.

CHICKEN UDON NOODLE SOUP

DAIRY-FREE | NUT-FREE | SUGAR-FREE | 1548 KJ/370 CAL PER SERVE

1 litre (35 fl oz/4 cups) chicken stock

1 thumb-size knob of ginger, peeled and sliced

4 button or shiitake mushrooms, sliced

1 dried chilli, crumbled

2 teaspoons soy sauce

1 teaspoon sesame oil

250 g (9 oz) chicken breast, finely sliced

2 celery sticks, sliced

200 g (7 oz) udon noodles

2 French shallots, finely sliced

1 bunch bok choy (pak choy), halved lengthways

handful of fresh mint and coriander (cilantro) leaves, to serve

2 lime wedges, to serve

Dressing (optional)

1 tablespoon crushed chilli flakes (or more, to taste)

2 tablespoons sesame oil

Pour the chicken stock into a large heavy-based saucepan with a lid. Add the ginger, mushrooms, chilli, soy sauce and sesame oil and bring to the boil. Turn the stock down to a simmer, add the chicken and the celery, put the lid on and let it simmer gently for approximately 8 minutes.

Place the udon noodles in hot water until they separate. Drain and add the noodles to the stock with the shallots and bok choy, then turn up the heat. When the soup comes to the boil, divide it between two bowls.

Top with mint and coriander leaves, and serve with lime wedges on the side. If you like your udon soup spicy, then mix the ingredients for the dressing together and serve on top of the cooked soup.

SERVES 2

TARTS 3 WAYS

NF | SF | V
1192 KJ/285 CAL PER SERVE

ASPARAGUS & RICOTTA TART

1 sheet frozen puff pastry, thawed

200 g (7 oz) white asparagus, trimmed

200 g (7 oz) green asparagus, trimmed

450 g (1 lb) fresh ricotta cheese

35 g (1¼ oz/¼ cup) finely grated romano or parmesan cheese

2 eggs (free-range, organic)

1 tablespoon finely chopped flat-leaf (Italian) parsley

1 tablespoon thyme leaves

sea salt and cracked black pepper

30 g (1 oz) butter, melted, for brushing

Special equipment

34 × 12 cm (13½ × 5 inch) fluted tart tin

Preheat the oven to 200°C (430°F). Grease a tart tin and trim the pastry sheet to fit the tin, ensuring the edges are covered. Fold up 1 cm (⅜ inch) on each edge. Using a fork, make small pricks in the base of the pastry, cover with baking paper and weigh it down with baking beans. Bake for around 10 minutes, then remove.

Cut the asparagus into 10 cm (4 inch) lengths. Finely chop any remaining asparagus and reserve for the filling.

To make the filling, process the cheeses and the eggs in a food processor until smooth. Transfer the mixture to a bowl and stir through the chopped parsley, thyme, reserved asparagus and salt and pepper.

Spoon the mixture into the pastry shell and arrange the lengths of asparagus on top, alternating the colours. Brush the pastry border with the melted butter.

Bake for 20 minutes or until golden and crispy on the edge.

SERVES 6

NF | SF | V
1247 KJ/298 CAL PER SERVE

ROSEMARY TOMATO TART WITH CREAMED GOAT'S CHEESE

24 cm (9½ inch) square sheet frozen puff pastry, thawed

4 large roma (plum) tomatoes, sliced

2 rosemary sprigs, leaves picked

1 egg (free-range, organic), beaten

1 teaspoon extra virgin olive oil for oiling and brushing

45 g (1½ oz/⅓ cup) soft goat's cheese

85 g (3 oz/⅓ cup) crème fraîche

rocket (arugula) leaves, to serve (optional)

Preheat the oven to 200°C (430°F).

Line a baking tray with baking paper and lay the sheet of puff pastry on the tray. Fold up 1 cm (⅜ inch) on each edge to make a small lip. Using a fork, make small pricks in the base of the pastry, cover with baking paper and weigh it down with baking beans, beans or similar. Bake in the oven for around 10 minutes, then remove.

Arrange the tomato slices over the pastry.

Sprinkle the tomato with rosemary leaves, a little sea salt and ground black pepper.

Brush the pastry border generously with beaten egg, then brush the tomatoes with a little oil and bake for 20 minutes or until the pastry is golden.

Meanwhile, put the goat's cheese and crème fraîche in a small bowl and whisk to combine. Serve each slice of tart topped with a dollop of creamed goat's cheese and rocket leaves, if using.

SERVES 4

NF | V
1289 KJ/308 CAL PER SERVE

GOAT'S CHEESE & CARAMELISED ONION TART

3 brown onions, thinly sliced

1 tablespoon olive oil

2 tablespoons brown sugar

2 tablespoons vinegar

1 sheet frozen puff pastry, thawed

1 thyme sprig, leaves picked

100 g (3½ oz/¾ cup) goat's cheese

1 egg (free-range, organic), beaten (optional)

Preheat the oven to 200°C (400°F). Line a baking tray with baking paper and set aside.

Caramelise the onions by frying them in olive oil in a frying pan over low heat for 3–5 minutes or until browned. Add brown sugar and vinegar and stir for another 8–10 minutes or until softened. Remove from heat and set aside.

Cut the pastry into four and place each piece on the prepared baking tray. Score a line 1 cm (⅜ inch) in from the edges and prick the centre of each quarter all over with a fork. Smear inside the scored lines with the onion and its cooking juices. Sprinkle on a few fresh thyme leaves. Scatter small pieces of goat's cheese over and bake for 15 minutes or until the pastry is golden and cooked. If you like, brush the exposed pastry edges with a beaten egg.

SERVES 4

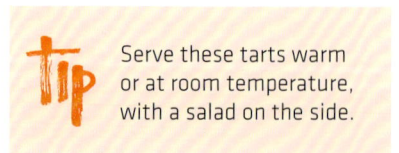

TIP Serve these tarts warm or at room temperature, with a salad on the side.

the GOOD life

CAULIFLOWER SOUP

GLUTEN-FREE | NUT-FREE | PALEO | SUGAR-FREE | VEGETARIAN | 653 KJ/156 CAL PER SERVE

1 tablespoon oil

1 brown onion, diced

1 leek (white and pale green parts only), thinly sliced

3 garlic cloves, minced

1 head of cauliflower, chopped into florets

1 litre (35 fl oz/4 cups) chicken or vegetable stock

65 g (2½ oz/¼ cup) light sour cream (optional), to serve

2 teaspoons olive oil, to serve

Heat the oil in a large saucepan over medium heat and cook the onion, leek and garlic, stirring frequently until softened and fragrant. Add the cauliflower, a pinch of salt (or more, to taste), and the stock, increasing to medium–high heat and bringing it to a simmer.

Once simmering, reduce the heat to medium–low, cover with a lid, and leave to cook for around 20 minutes or longer, until the cauliflower is tender.

When cooked, remove from the heat and use a handblender to process until smooth. Alternatively, carefully transfer the soup in batches to an upright blender and blend until smooth. Taste and adjust seasoning with salt and freshly ground black pepper.

Pour back into the pot to reheat slightly over low heat.

Serve with a dollop of sour cream (if using) and a few dots of olive oil.

SERVES 4

tip This soup can also be topped with a few dots of pesto and is delicious served with crusty bread.

live
love
cook
eat

#TheGoodLife

CHICKEN SAN CHOY BOW

DAIRY-FREE | GLUTEN-FREE | NUT-FREE | SUGAR-FREE | 1640 KJ/392 CAL PER SERVE

4 large iceberg lettuce leaves (cups)

2 tablespoons olive oil

1 brown onion, diced

1 carrot, diced

3 spring onions (scallions), thinly sliced

1 garlic clove, minced

1 teaspoon grated ginger

500 g (1 lb 2 oz) minced (ground) chicken

2 tablespoons Chinese rice wine

225 g (8¼ oz) tin of water chestnuts (available at supermarkets or Asian grocery stores), drained

230 g (8¼ oz) tin sliced bamboo shoots (available at supermarkets or Asian grocery stores), drained

¼ cup soy sauce or tamari

2 tablespoons honey or rice malt syrup

1 tablespoon cornflour (cornstarch)

1 tablespoon chopped coriander (cilantro) leaves

2 teaspoons sesame seeds, to serve

Put the lettuce leaf cups into a bowl of iced water. Set aside.

Heat the olive oil in a frying pan or wok over high heat. Add the onion, carrot and 2 of the spring onions, stirring frequently until softened and lightly browned. Add the garlic and ginger and continue to stir. Add the chicken, breaking it up with a wooden spoon or fork to ensure that the texture and cooking is even. Add a little more oil to the pan if the chicken is sticking.

Once the chicken has browned, add the Chinese rice wine, then scrape the bottom of the pan to lift up the caramelised flavours.

Add the water chestnuts and bamboo shoots. Continue to stir. If the mixture begins to stick, turn the heat down to medium. Add the soy sauce (or tamari) and honey (or rice malt syrup, if using) and stir.

In a separate bowl or mixing jug, add the cornflour to 60 ml (2 fl oz/¼ cup) of water, and stir until combined. Add to the pan and stir thoroughly. Cook for a few minutes until the chicken is cooked and the sauce has thickened. If the sauce looks too dry, then add a splash more water.

Taste, and season with salt and pepper if required. If it's too salty, then add a small drizzle of honey (or rice malt syrup). To deepen the flavours, add another 60 ml (2 fl oz/¼ cup) of soy sauce (or tamari) and 2 tablespoons of honey (or rice malt syrup). Remove from heat once the flavour has developed. Stir through the coriander.

Drain the lettuce and allow to dry. Divide the chicken mixture evenly between the lettuce cups, top with the dark green slices of the remaining spring onion and sprinkle with sesame seeds.

SERVES 4

LUNCH

LAMB CUTLETS WITH DIPPING SAUCE

GLUTEN-FREE | NUT-FREE | SUGAR-FREE | 799 KJ/191 CAL PER SERVE

8 lamb cutlets, fat trimmed

1 tablespoon ground cumin

1 teaspoon smoked paprika

½ teaspoon garlic powder

½ teaspoon of ground chilli (optional)

1 tablespoon olive oil

a few leaves of fresh coriander (cilantro), to serve

Dipping sauce

130 g (4½ oz/½ cup) plain yoghurt

zest and juice of ½ small lemon

1 garlic clove, minced

5 g (¼ oz/¼ cup) mint leaves, finely chopped, plus extra mint leaves to serve

For the cutlets, combine the cumin, paprika, garlic, chilli (if using) and olive oil in a bowl. Mix to combine. Add salt and freshly ground black pepper to taste. Put the cutlets in the bowl and rub evenly with the spice mix to coat all sides.

Make the dipping sauce by combining all of the ingredients and stirring gently with a fork. Season with salt to taste, then sprinkle with a few extra mint leaves on top. Set aside.

Heat a barbecue or chargrill to high and cook the cutlets for 2 minutes on each side or until cooked to your liking. Transfer to a plate and set aside to rest for 3–5 minutes.

Once rested, serve cutlets with the fresh coriander and dipping sauce.

SERVES 4

tips

- The dipping sauce can be made ahead of time and kept in the fridge. The cutlets can also be prepared ahead of time, covered and kept in the fridge. Remove from the fridge around 30–45 minutes before cooking.
- Serve with a side of grilled lemons and lightly grilled vine-ripened cherry tomatoes.

the GOOD life

CHICKEN SALAD IN A JAR 3 WAYS

DF | SF
1966 KJ/470 CAL PER SERVE

(LEAN) (FAST)

ASIAN CHICKEN NOODLE SALAD

120 g (4¼ oz) soba noodles

2 small barbecue chicken breasts, skin removed, shredded into chunks

1 large carrot, peeled and grated

5 g (¼ oz/¼ cup) mint leaves, roughly chopped

1 red capsicum (pepper), thinly sliced

4 spring onions (scallions), thinly sliced

½ small red oakleaf or cos lettuce, shredded

115 g (4 oz/1 cup) bean sprouts

7 g (¼ oz/¼ cup) coriander (cilantro) leaves, roughly chopped

Spicy peanut dressing

2 tablespoons peanut butter

1 tablespoon sambal oelek (chilli paste)

1 tablespoon rice vinegar

1 tablespoon soy sauce

60 ml (2 fl oz/¼ cup) extra virgin olive oil

1 tablespoon black sesame seeds

Cook soba noodles according to package instructions. Rinse under cold water and drain.

Make the dressing in a small bowl, whisking together peanut butter, sambal oelek, rice vinegar and soy sauce. While whisking, slowly drizzle in the olive oil. Stir in the sesame seeds.

To assemble, divide the dressing equally among 4 large-size Mason (preserving) jars. Add the chicken, so it absorbs the flavour of the sauce, then the carrot, mint, soba noodles, capsicum, spring onion, lettuce, bean sprouts and coriander. Seal the jars and refrigerate. To serve, pour the contents of a jar onto a plate or bowl, stir and enjoy.

MAKES 4 JARS

SF
4782 KJ/1143 CAL PER SERVE

(FAB) (FAST)

CHICKEN, PEAR & PECAN SALAD

½ small barbecue chicken, skin removed, shredded into chunks

60 g (2¼ oz/½ cup) roughly chopped pecan nuts

1 pear, cored and thinly sliced

½ red (Spanish) onion, thinly sliced

2 cups mixed salad leaves

60 g (2¼ oz) blue cheese or goat's cheese, crumbled

40 g (1½ oz/¼ cup) dried cranberries

Maple cider vinaigrette

60 ml (2 fl oz/¼ cup) olive oil

60 ml (2 fl oz/¼ cup) apple cider vinegar

2 tablespoons maple syrup or rice malt syrup

2 tablespoons dijon mustard

To make the vinaigrette, mix all of the ingredients together and season to taste with salt and pepper.

To assemble, divide the dressing between the two jars, then add half the chicken, pecans, pear slices, red onion and mixed salad leaves to each jar. Top each jar with crumbled cheese and cranberries. Seal the jars and refrigerate. To serve, pour the contents of a jar onto a plate or bowl, stir and enjoy.

MAKES 2 JARS

DF | NF
1661 KJ/397 CAL PER SERVE

(LEAN) (FAST)

THAI CHOPPED CHICKEN SALAD WITH CHILLI DRESSING

1 small barbecue chicken, skin removed, shredded into chunks

60 g (2 oz/1 cup) small broccoli florets

½ red cabbage, finely shredded

½ cos lettuce, finely shredded

2 Lebanese (short) cucumbers, julienned

1 mango, peeled and chopped into chunks

Dressing

juice of 4 limes

2 tablespoons fish sauce

½ teaspoon minced garlic

2 tablespoons caster (superfine) sugar

2 bird's eye chillies, seeded and finely chopped

¼ teaspoon grated ginger

To make the dressing, whisk all of the ingredients together until the sugar has dissolved.

To assemble, divide the dressing between 4 Mason (preserving) jars, then divide and add the chicken, broccoli, cabbage, cos lettuce, cucumber and mango. Seal the jars and refrigerate. To serve, pour the contents of a jar onto a plate or bowl, stir and enjoy.

MAKES 4 JARS

TIP These salads will keep in the fridge until the next day but are best eaten on the same day. Serve them at room temperature.

GRILLED CORN & AVOCADO TOASTIE

NUT-FREE | SUGAR-FREE | VEGETARIAN | 3602 KJ/861 CAL PER SERVE

2 corncobs

1 tablespoon olive oil

2 tablespoons unsalted butter, softened

½ teaspoon Cajun spice seasoning

4 slices sourdough bread

2 small avocados, peeled, stones removed

juice of ¼ lemon or lime

2 tablespoons coarsely chopped fresh coriander (cilantro) leaves, 1 tablespoon extra leaves to serve

50 g (¾ oz/⅓ cup) crumbled Danish feta cheese

To grill the corn, brush or rub the corncobs with the olive oil. Put the cobs on the grill (broiler) and cook until golden or charred—whichever you prefer—turning the ears to cook evenly. Remove them from the grill and allow to cool slightly.

Mix together the butter, Cajun spice seasoning and some salt and pepper. Slice the corn kernels off the cob and toss in the butter mixture.

Toast the sourdough slices. While the bread is toasting, mash the avocados with the lemon or lime juice and stir through a generous pinch of salt and pepper and the chopped coriander.

Spread the avocado smash on the toast then top with corn kernels and crumbled feta. Garnish with coriander.

SERVES 2

BEEF WONTON SOUP

DAIRY-FREE | NUT-FREE | SUGAR-FREE | 1770 KJ/423 CAL PER SERVE

250 g (9 oz) minced (ground) lean beef

1 clove garlic, minced

1 teaspoon salt

1 teaspoon pepper

1 teaspoon Chinese five spice

5 spring onions (scallions), chopped

1 teaspoon sesame oil

3 cm (1¼ inch) piece of ginger, peeled and finely chopped

½ of a 225 g (8¼ oz) tin water chestnuts, drained and finely chopped

270 g (9½ oz) packet square wonton wrappers

750 ml (26 fl oz/3 cups) chicken stock

1 bunch bok choy (pak choy)

½ bunch coriander (cilantro), leaves torn

For the sauce

1 tablespoon light soy sauce (or tamari)

1 teaspoon sesame seeds

1 teaspoon rice vinegar

2 teaspoons chilli oil (optional)

In a large bowl, mix together the beef, garlic, salt, pepper, Chinese five spice, 2 chopped spring onions and the sesame oil. Set aside for the flavours to develop. Add the ginger and water chestnuts to the beef mixture to make the filling.

Meanwhile, mix the ingredients for the sauce together.

Place 2 teaspoons of the beef mixture in the centre of each wonton wrapper and fold the corners to the middle to enclose the filling. Wet the edges of the wrapper with a finger dipped in water to seal.

Place the stock and 1 cup of water in a large saucepan and bring to the boil. Cook the wontons in batches, for about 2–5 minutes. Add the bok choy for 1 minute.

Scoop the stock from the saucepan into serving bowls to make the soup base and divide the wontons between the plates. Pour the sauce over the wontons and soup and stir gently. Sprinkle with the remaining chopped spring onion and the coriander.

SERVES 4

SARDINES WITH PRESERVED LEMON

DAIRY-FREE | NUT-FREE | SUGAR-FREE | 1602 KJ/383 CAL PER SERVE

60 g (2¼ oz/1 cup) panko (Japanese) breadcrumbs

2 garlic cloves, minced

15 g (½ oz/½ cup) coarsely chopped flat-leaf (Italian) parsley

2 tablespoons finely grated lemon zest

2 tablespoons olive oil, plus extra, to drizzle

12 sardines, about 400 g (14 oz), cleaned and gutted

Preserved lemon salsa

15 g (½ oz/½ cup) coarsely chopped flat-leaf (Italian) parsley

2 preserved lemons, seeded and finely chopped

2 garlic cloves, minced

2 tablespoons olive oil olive

Preheat the oven to 200°C (400°F). Line a baking tray with baking paper and set aside.

Mix breadcrumbs with garlic, parsley, lemon zest and olive oil, and season with salt and pepper.

Put a generous amount of breadcrumb mixture into each sardine. Reserve the remaining breadcrumb mixture.

Put the sardines on the prepared baking tray. Pour a generous drizzle of olive oil over the sardines. Roast, uncovered, for 15–20 minutes. Sprinkle with the reserved breadcrumb mixture for the last 5 minutes of cooking.

Meanwhile, make the preserved lemon salsa by combining all of the ingredients in a small bowl.

Serve the sardines with the preserved lemon salsa and a side salad, if desired.

SERVES 4

QUICK & EASY QUESADILLAS 2 WAYS

NF | SF
2753 KJ/658 CAL PER SERVE

CHICKEN & FETA QUESADILLAS

1 tablespoon olive oil

2 spring onions (scallions), chopped

2 light tortillas

75 g (2¾ oz/½ cup) shredded light mozzarella cheese

90 g (3¼ oz/2 cups) baby spinach leaves

1 small grilled chicken breast, skin removed, meat shredded

65 g (2¼ oz/½ cup) feta cheese, crumbled

65 g (2¼ oz/¼ cup) light sour cream, to serve

Salsa

16 cherry tomatoes, quartered

½ red (Spanish) onion, finely chopped

1 tablespoon finely chopped coriander (cilantro) leaves

juice of ½ a lime

pinch of chilli powder (optional)

Combine the salsa ingredients together in a bowl, season with salt and freshly ground black pepper and set aside.

Heat the olive oil in a frying pan over medium heat. Add the spring onion, stirring for a few minutes until softened. Remove from the pan and set aside.

Put a tortilla into the pan and lightly brown on both sides. Sprinkle half of the mozzarella across the entire tortilla. On one half of the tortilla, put half of the spinach, half of the chicken, half of the spring onion, and half of the feta.

Fold the tortilla in half, press down and cook for a couple of minutes. Flip the tortilla carefully and cook the other side for another minute or two.

Repeat with the remaining tortilla and filling ingredients.

Cut each quesadilla in half. Serve with the light sour cream and salsa.

SERVES 2

NF | SF | V
2807 KJ/671 CAL PER SERVE

KALE & SMASHED BEANS QUESADILLAS

1 tablespoon olive oil

½ small red (Spanish) onion, sliced

2 kale leaves, stalks removed and leaves roughly chopped

400 g (14 oz) tin of cannellini beans, drained and rinsed

2 light tortillas

130 g (4½ oz/1 cup) shredded light mozzarella cheese

8 cherry tomatoes, chopped

Smoky yoghurt sauce

130 g (4½ oz/½ cup) low-fat natural yoghurt

2 tablespoons barbecue sauce (or use ½ teaspoon smoked paprika, 1 teaspoon lemon juice and a pinch of salt)

Heat the olive oil in a frying pan over medium heat and cook the onion, stirring, for 2 minutes. Add the kale, season with salt and pepper and cook for a further 1–2 minutes. Next, add the beans and cook for a few minutes or until the onion and kale have softened.

Transfer the mixture to a bowl. Using a fork, mash the beans, then taste and adjust seasoning if required.

Return the frying pan to the stovetop over low heat. Lightly brown one tortilla on both sides. Sprinkle half of the mozzarella across the tortilla. Spread half of the bean mix across half of the tortilla and top with half of the chopped tomato.

Fold the tortilla in half, press down and cook for a couple of minutes. Flip the tortilla and cook the other side for another minute or two. Repeat with the remaining tortilla and filling ingredients.

Mix together the sauce ingredients in a small bowl. Cut each quesadilla in half and serve with the smoky sauce.

SERVES 2

SUPERFOOD SUPERSALAD

GLUTEN-FREE | SUGAR-FREE | VEGETARIAN | 2297 KJ/549 CAL PER SERVE

1 large carrot, peeled, diced

1 medium zucchini (courgette), diced

25 g (1 oz/1 cup) baby kale leaves (stalks removed, leaves sliced)

45 g (1½ oz/1 cup) baby spinach leaves

1 cup silverbeet (Swiss chard), stalks removed, leaves sliced

1 cup broccoli, chopped into florets

1 cup cauliflower, chopped into florets

8 Brussels sprouts, blanched and sliced

1 red capsicum (pepper), seeded, sliced

250 g (9 oz/1 punnet) cherry tomatoes, halved

1 small avocado, peeled, stone removed, cubed

1 small sweet potato, cubed, steamed

60 g (2¼ oz/½ cup) walnuts

4 tablespoons black and white chia seeds

handful each of basil and mint leaves, finely chopped

Dressing

90 g (3¼ oz/⅓ cup) unhulled tahini

95 g (3¼ oz/⅓ cup) natural yoghurt

60 ml (2 fl oz/¼ cup) lemon juice

2 garlic cloves, minced

1 teaspoon honey or rice malt syrup

Put the vegetables, avocado, walnuts, chia seeds and herbs in a large serving bowl and toss to combine.

Whisk together dressing ingredients and season with salt and pepper to taste.

Divide the vegetables among plates and serve with the dressing.

SERVES 4

SPICY LAMB FLATBREADS

NUT-FREE | SUGAR-FREE | 2033 KJ/486 CAL PER SERVE

1 tablespoon olive oil

1 brown onion, finely chopped

1 spring onion (scallion), finely chopped

1 garlic clove, finely chopped

1 teaspoon ground coriander

1 teaspoon ground cumin

1 tablespoon baharat (Middle Eastern spice mix)

500 g (1 lb 2 oz) minced (ground) lean lamb

2 green chillies, finely chopped

300 ml (10½ fl oz/1¼ cups) chicken stock

40 g (1½ oz/½ bunch) mint

250 g (9 oz/1 cup) plain yoghurt

4 rounds of Lebanese bread

oil spray

90 g (3¼ oz/1 bunch) coriander (cilantro), leaves picked

lemon wedges, to serve

Heat a frying pan over medium heat and put in the oil, onion, spring onion, garlic and spices, then fry for 2 minutes. Add the lamb and cook over high heat, turning often and breaking up with a wooden spoon, until the meat is browned all over.

Add the chilli and chicken stock and bring to the boil, then reduce the heat and simmer for 20 minutes or until the mince is tender and the stock has nearly all evaporated. Taste and season with salt and pepper, then leave to cool.

Preheat the oven to 200°C (400°F). Finely shred half of the mint and mix it with the yoghurt and a generous pinch of salt.

Spray the Lebanese bread with oil spray and lay the rounds on a baking tray. Bake for 5–10 minutes or until golden and crisp. Top with the warm lamb mixture and a dollop of yoghurt, scatter with the remaining mint leaves and the coriander, and serve with the rest of the mint yoghurt plus lemon wedges.

SERVES 4

Tips
• Squeeze lemon juice over the top just before eating.
• You could also use mountain bread or pitta bread.

CHICKEN, KALE & LEMON SOUP

DAIRY-FREE | NUT-FREE | SUGAR-FREE | 1494 KJ/357 CAL PER SERVE

1 medium free-range chicken

2 brown onions, quartered

2 leeks (white and pale green parts only), sliced into 1.5 cm (⁵⁄₈ inch) slices

2 celery stalks, chopped into thirds

2 carrots, chopped into quarters

6 garlic cloves, peeled and halved

2 bay leaves

1–2 tablespoons sea salt

1 teaspoon freshly ground black pepper

165 g (5¾ oz/¾ cup) risoni pasta

100 g (3½ oz/4 cups) kale ribbons (stalks removed, leaves sliced)

zest and juice of 2 lemons

1 tablespoon chopped flat-leaf (Italian) parsley or dill, to serve

Put the chicken, onion, leek, celery, carrot, garlic and bay leaves in a large saucepan or stock pot and season with sea salt and freshly ground black pepper. Cover the chicken with water, bring to a boil and then reduce the heat slightly, leaving it to simmer for about 60 minutes or until the chicken is cooked through.

Transfer the chicken to a plate and let it stand until it's just cool enough to handle. Remove the skin and discard, pull the meat off the chicken, shred it into bite-size pieces and put them in a bowl.

Meanwhile, use a slotted spoon to remove the remaining ingredients from the stock pot. Transfer them to a bowl (you can eat the carrots and onions from this mix later—they're delicious!).

Add the risoni and kale to the simmering liquid, cooking until the risoni is al dente (around 10 minutes).

Return the shredded chicken to the soup and add the lemon zest and juice, stirring through to warm. Taste and adjust seasoning if required. Stir through the chopped parsley or dill and serve immediately.

SERVES 6

RAINBOW SILVERBEET WITH SLIVERED ALMONDS

DAIRY-FREE | GLUTEN-FREE | PALEO | SUGAR-FREE | VEGAN | 1226 KJ/293 CAL PER SERVE

45 g (1½ oz/⅓ cup) slivered almonds

2 tablespoons olive oil

2 garlic cloves, minced

1 brown onion, chopped

2 kg (4 lb 8 oz/2 bunches) rainbow silverbeet (Swiss chard), stems sliced and reserved, leaves sliced

75 g (2¾ oz/½ cup) dried cranberries

zest of ½ lemon

1 tablespoon lemon juice, plus extra to taste

Toast the almonds in a frying pan over medium–high heat. Once they begin to develop a golden-brown colour, remove from the heat and transfer to a bowl.

Heat 1 tablespoon of olive oil in the pan over medium–high heat and sauté garlic, onion and silverbeet stems until softened. Add the silverbeet leaves and stir until softened.

Remove from the heat, add the cranberries and almonds, lemon zest, lemon juice and the remaining tablespoon of olive oil. Season with salt and freshly ground black pepper.

Toss to combine and serve.

SERVES 4

LICK THE PLATE LAMB SOUVLAKI

GLUTEN-FREE | NUT-FREE | SUGAR-FREE | 2628 KJ/628 CAL PER SERVE

60 ml (2 fl oz/¼ cup) olive oil

2 tablespoons coarsely chopped thyme

2 tablespoons coarsely chopped flat-leaf (Italian) parsley

1 teaspoon dried oregano

2 garlic cloves, crushed

juice of 1 lemon

800 g (1 lb 12 oz) boneless lamb leg roast, trimmed, cut into 3 cm (1¼ inch) chunks

1 red capsicum (pepper), cut into 3 cm (1¼ inch) pieces

1 red (Spanish) onion, cut into 3 cm (1¼ inch) pieces

1 green capsicum (pepper) cut into 3 cm (1¼ inch) pieces

olive oil (optional), to serve

4 lemons, halved, to serve

8 small tortillas (optional), to serve

sprinkle of salt and oregano (optional), to serve

Tzatziki

1 Lebanese (short) cucumber, finely grated (squeeze out and discard excess moisture)

2 garlic cloves, minced

500 g (1 lb 2 oz) Greek-style yoghurt

2 tablespoons finely chopped mint

mint leaves, extra, for garnish

In a large bowl, combine the oil with the herbs, garlic and lemon juice. Season with salt and pepper. Add the lamb and toss to coat. Cover and refrigerate for 2–4 hours, overnight for a stronger flavour.

Thread the red capsicum, onion, green capsicum and lamb cubes alternately onto skewers.

Heat a large frying pan or barbecue plate to medium. Cook the lamb for 15–20 minutes or until crispy on all sides.

Make the tzatziki by combining all of the ingredients. Transfer to a serving bowl and garnish with extra mint leaves.

Lightly brush the tortillas (if using) with olive oil and sprinkle with salt. Heat a chargrill pan over low–medium heat, brush with oil and lay a tortilla in the pan, flipping once until heated through. Alternatively, warm the tortillas in a preheated oven for about 4 minutes.

Serve souvlaki with tzatziki, tortillas (if using) and halved lemons on a big wooden chopping board.

SERVES 4

dinner

CAULIFLOWER CRUST PIZZA

GLUTEN-FREE | NUT-FREE | SUGAR-FREE | 2138 KJ/511 CAL PER SERVE

1 large cauliflower, grated or blended into 'rice' with a food processor or blender, to make about 4 cups

3 eggs (free-range, organic), lightly beaten

1 teaspoon dried oregano

1 tablespoon Italian seasoning

80 g (2¾ oz/¾ cup) almond meal

4 tablespoons grated parmesan cheese

1 tablespoon salt

1 teaspoon pepper

Topping

125–185 g (4½–6½ oz/½–¾ cup) tomato passata or tomato paste

125 g (4½ oz/1 cup) grated mozzarella cheese

1 chorizo sausage, thinly sliced

250 g (9 oz/1 punnet) cherry tomatoes, halved

50 g (1¾ oz/⅓ cup) goat's cheese, crumbled

15 g (½ oz/½ cup) basil leaves

Preheat the oven to 200°C (400°F).

Put the cauliflower 'rice' into a microwave-safe bowl and microwave for 8–10 minutes on High or until the cauliflower becomes tender. Drain and set aside to cool. Tip the cauliflower into the middle of a tea towel (dish towel). Wrap it into a bundle, and twist closed, squeezing out any remaining moisture over the sink. You need a proper pizza base, not a crumbly mess.

Transfer the drained cauliflower to a large bowl and add the eggs, oregano, Italian seasoning, almond meal, parmesan cheese and salt and pepper. Fold the mixture—or use your hands to mix the dough—until it is well combined. If it's still a bit too runny, add another tablespoon of almond meal to firm it up.

Heat a nonstick pizza tray or baking tray for 5–10 minutes, then spread the 'dough' out in a layer 5 mm (¼ inch) thick. Bake the 'dough' for 15 minutes or until it becomes golden. Remove from the oven (but leave the oven on).

Spread the tomato passata or paste evenly over the base, followed by the grated mozzarella, chorizo and cherry tomato. Scatter the crumbled goat's cheese in between the chorizo and tomato, then sprinkle with the basil leaves. Return to the oven and cook for a further 5–10 minutes or until the cheese has melted.

SERVES 4

tip Replace the toppings or add to them with other toppings of your choice: we love baby spinach, spicy merguez sausage and pitted kalamata olives.

SEARED BEEF WITH SOBA NOODLE SALAD

DAIRY-FREE | NUT-FREE | SUGAR-FREE | 2494 KJ/596 CAL PER SERVE

1 tablespoon olive oil

300 g (10½ oz) eye fillet or rump steak

50 g (1¾ oz) shiitake mushrooms, finely sliced

50 g (1¾ oz/1 cup) baby spinach leaves

150 g (5½ oz) soba noodles

100 g (3½ oz) snow peas (mangetout), trimmed

½ tablespoon soy sauce (or tamari)

1 tablespoon mirin seasoning

2 spring onions (scallions) (green part only), cut into strips, to serve

Put the olive oil in a frying pan and bring to high heat. Season the beef with salt and pepper and add to the pan, cooking for 2 minutes each side, or until cooked to your liking. Remove from the pan, cover and allow to rest.

Return the pan to the stovetop, add the mushrooms and stir until softened. Add the baby spinach to the mushrooms and stir until the leaves have wilted. Remove from the heat.

Cook the noodles according to the packet instructions. Add the snow peas to the saucepan during the last 2 minutes of cooking time.

While that's cooking, make the dressing by combining the soy sauce (or tamari, if using) and mirin in a bowl, mixing well. Set aside.

Drain the noodles and snow peas. Transfer them to a large bowl and mix together with the mushrooms, baby spinach and dressing. Toss to combine.

Divide the noodles and vegies between two bowls. Slice the steak thinly, lay it on top of the noodles, top with spring onion, and serve.

SERVES 2

NO NOODLE PAD THAI

DAIRY-FREE | SUGAR-FREE | VEGETARIAN | 2243 KJ/536 CAL PER SERVE

2 carrots

2 medium zucchini (courgettes)

150 g (5½ oz) long white radishes (optional)

3 spring onions (scallions), finely sliced

115 g (4 oz/1 cup) bean sprouts

7 g (¼ oz/¼ cup) coriander (cilantro) leaves, chopped, plus extra whole leaves, to serve

140 g (5 oz/¾ cup) firm tofu, drained

2 tablespoons sesame seeds, toasted

1 lime, quartered, to serve

Sauce

2 tablespoons soy sauce (or tamari)

1 tablespoon honey (or agave syrup)

1 teaspoon grated ginger

1 garlic clove, minced

2 tablespoons lime juice

¼ cup peanut butter (or your choice of nut butter)

½ long red chilli, deseeded and finely chopped

Use a spiraliser or a vegetable peeler to make 'noodles' or ribbons from the carrots, zucchini and radishes. Put them in a large bowl with the spring onion, bean sprouts and coriander, and toss to combine.

Dice the tofu into 1.5 cm (⅝ inch) cubes and add to the bowl with the vegies.

Make the sauce by whisking together the ingredients until smooth. Taste and adjust with a little extra soy sauce or lime juice if required. Pour the dressing over the vegies and gently mix to combine.

To serve, sprinkle with sesame seeds and top with extra coriander leaves and 2 lime quarters.

SERVES 2

tips
- Prepare both the vegies and the sauce in advance, then store them separately. Only mix them together at serving time.
- Don't feel like tofu? Try switching it up for a scrambled egg.

WHOLE BAKED SNAPPER WITH SALSA VERDE

DAIRY-FREE | GLUTEN-FREE | NUT-FREE | PALEO | SUGAR-FREE | 1602 KJ/383 CAL PER SERVE

1 x 1 kg (2 lb 4 oz) whole snapper (ask your fishmonger to clean and scale the fish for you)

60 ml (2 fl oz/¼ cup) olive oil

3 lemons, halved and sliced

4 garlic cloves, sliced thinly

3 long red chilli, sliced (use more or less, to taste)

Salsa verde

60 ml (2 fl oz/¼ cup) olive oil

60 g (2 oz/1 cup) finely chopped flat-leaf (Italian) parsley

20 g (¾ oz/⅓ cup) chopped chives

1 tablespoon baby capers in brine, rinsed and chopped

2 garlic cloves, minced

1 teaspoon dijon mustard

1 tablespoon red wine vinegar

Preheat the oven to 200°C (400°F).

Score the fish on both sides. Drizzle a little of the olive oil on a baking dish. Lay the fish in the baking dish. Drizzle with the remaining olive oil and season well on each side with salt and pepper.

Fill the cuts in the fish with half the lemon slices, all of the garlic and half the chilli (if using). Lay the remaining lemon slices and chilli on top of the fish and in the baking dish.

Bake the fish for around 30 minutes or until the flesh is firm and opaque when it is flaked with a fork.

Meanwhile, make the salsa verde by mixing all of the ingredients in a small bowl. Season to taste with salt and pepper.

Serve the snapper in the baking dish with the salsa verde on the side.

SERVES 4

SKILLET LASAGNE

NUT-FREE | SUGAR-FREE | 3636 KJ/869 CAL PER SERVE

500 g (1 lb 2 oz) merguez or chorizo sausages, or similar

2 tablespoons olive oil

1 onion, finely minced

4 garlic cloves, crushed

2 × 400 g (14 oz) tins crushed tomatoes

15 g (½ oz/¼ cup) chopped basil leaves, plus a handful of basil leaves, extra, to serve

1 teaspoon dried oregano

230 g (8¼ oz/1 cup) fresh ricotta cheese

20 g (¾ oz/¼ cup) shredded parmesan cheese

1 egg (free-range, organic), beaten

200 g (7 oz) fresh lasagne sheets

250 g (9 oz) buffalo mozzarella cheese, thinly sliced

Slice sausage into 1 cm (⅜ inch) slices. Heat the olive oil in a deep ovenproof skillet with a 2 litre (70 fl oz/8 cup) capacity and a lid. Add the sausage and fry until cooked through. Remove the sausage from the skillet and set aside.

Reduce the heat to medium–low. Add the onion and garlic with some salt and pepper and fry until the onion has softened. Add crushed tomatoes, basil and oregano and simmer for 10 minutes, stirring occasionally.

While the sauce simmers, mix the ricotta, parmesan and egg together with some salt and pepper. Cut the lasagne sheets to roughly fit your pan.

When the sauce has finished cooking, add the sliced sausage and stir well. Remove three-quarters of the sauce and reserve in a bowl, leaving a quarter of the sauce mixture in the skillet. Layer lasagne sheets over the sauce then top with a quarter of the ricotta mixture. Repeat so that you have sauce, then lasagne sheets, then ricotta layers until all the ingredients are covering the base of the pan, not neatly stacked. Cover the skillet with the lid and cook over low heat for 30 minutes.

Top with mozzarella slices and continue to simmer, covered, for about 2 minutes until the cheese is melted. Top with extra basil leaves before serving.

SERVES 4

tip Merguez sausage is a type of North African spicy lamb sausage, available from delis and specialty food stores.

QUICK CHICKEN LETTUCE WRAPS

DAIRY-FREE | NUT-FREE | SUGAR-FREE | 1272 KJ/304 CAL PER SERVE

1 tablespoon olive oil

1 garlic clove, minced

½ cooked chicken, skin removed and meat shredded (it's totally okay to use a ready-cooked barbecue chicken)

60 ml (2 fl oz/¼ cup) chicken stock

1 tablespoon soy sauce (or tamari)

2 teaspoons oyster sauce

2 teaspoons hoisin sauce

½ teaspoon stevia

2–3 carrots, shredded (enough to make 1 cup)

¼ red cabbage, shredded (enough to make 1 cup)

1 spring onion (scallion), chopped

½ iceberg or butter lettuce, leaves separated and washed

1 tablespoon chopped coriander (cilantro) leaves

Dressing

1 teaspoon rice wine vinegar

1 teaspoon sesame oil

1 teaspoon sesame seeds

Heat the olive oil in a frying pan over medium heat, add the garlic and stir gently. Once the garlic softens and develops a little colour, add the shredded chicken and stir. Reduce the heat to medium–low.

In a bowl, combine the chicken stock, soy sauce (or tamari, if using), oyster sauce, hoisin sauce and stevia, and use a fork to whisk gently. Add this to the pan with the chicken and stir to make sure that the chicken is well coated. You may need to increase the heat slightly. Keep cooking until the liquid has reduced. Remove from the heat and transfer the mixture to a serving bowl.

To make the dressing, in a small bowl, whisk together the rice wine vinegar, sesame oil and sesame seeds. Taste and season with salt and pepper.

Put the carrot, cabbage and spring onion in a serving bowl. Toss to combine. Drizzle with the dressing mixture.

Place the lettuce leaves on a serving platter. Add the chicken to the platter alongside the lettuce, and sprinkle with coriander. To eat, spoon chicken and slaw into a lettuce leaf, roll up and eat immediately.

SERVES 2

QUICK STICKS GINGER BEEF

DAIRY-FREE | GLUTEN-FREE | NUT-FREE | SUGAR-FREE | 1368 KJ/327 CAL PER SERVE

1 tablespoon olive oil

1 red (Spanish) onion, sliced

1 red capsicum (pepper), sliced

200 g (7 oz) green beans, ends trimmed

200 g (7 oz) bok choy (pak choy), leaves separated

3 garlic cloves, sliced

5 cm (2 inch) piece of ginger, peeled and cut into slivers

500 g (1 lb 2 oz) skirt steak, thinly sliced

40 g (1½ oz/¼ cup) sesame seeds

Sauce

2 tablespoons dry sherry

1 tablespoon soy sauce

½ teaspoon sambal oelek

In a small bowl, mix the ingredients for the sauce together and set aside.

In a nonstick frying pan, heat ½ tablespoon of the olive oil over high heat. Add the onion and capsicum and stir-fry until almost cooked through. Add the beans and cook for 2 minutes. Add the bok choy and cook for approximately another 2 minutes. Transfer the vegetables to a bowl.

Add the remaining ½ tablespoon oil to the pan. When it is hot, add the garlic and ginger and cook, stirring often, for about 30 seconds or until fragrant but not browned. Add the beef slices to the pan and stir-fry for approximately 1 minute or until just browned, so as to not dry out the steak.

Return the vegetables to the pan along with the sauce mixture and cook for 1 minute or until heated through. Serve topped with sesame seeds.

SERVES 4

ROAST HARISSA CHICKEN

DAIRY-FREE | GLUTEN-FREE | NUT-FREE | PALEO | SUGAR-FREE | 2159 KJ/516 CAL PER SERVE

2 tablespoons olive oil

4 chicken thigh cutlets (free-range, organic), skin on

55 g (2 oz/¼ cup) harissa paste (see our recipe on page 218 or use purchased harissa)

2 lemons, cut into wedges

2 medium cobs steamed corn, to serve

1 cup tzatziki (optional), to serve (see our recipe on page 219)

Preheat the oven to 200°C (400°F). Lightly grease a baking tray with olive oil. Rub the olive oil and harissa paste all over the chicken, including under the skin. Season with salt and pepper.

Put the chicken and the lemon wedges on the prepared tray and bake for around 50 minutes (or until done), turning over every 15–20 minutes, so that the skin side is up for the final 15–20 minutes of cooking.

Remove from the oven and leave to rest for 10 minutes.

Serve immediately with corn and tzatziki (if using).

SERVES 4

STICKY SPICED DUCK

DAIRY-FREE | GLUTEN-FREE | NUT-FREE | PALEO | SUGAR-FREE | 2950 KJ/705 CAL PER SERVE

4 duck breasts, skin on

2 teaspoons Chinese five spice

Sauce

1 long red chilli, seeded and finely chopped

small handful of mint leaves, shredded

2 tablespoons olive oil

1 tablespoon lemon juice

2 teaspoons honey or rice malt syrup

Pat the duck breasts with paper towel to dry. Score (slash in a criss-cross) the skin of the duck breasts.

Season each breast with sea salt, freshly ground black pepper and half a teaspoon of the Chinese five spice. Be generous with the salt on the skin side of the duck, as this will help the skin to become crispy when cooking.

Heat a large frying pan over medium heat and fry the duck breasts, skin side down, for 10–12 minutes or until the fat has rendered and the skin is crisp. Check it before the 10-minute mark, as the cooking time will vary depending on the size and thickness of the breasts. Turn the breasts over and cook for another 5 minutes or until browned.

Once the duck is cooked to your liking, remove from the pan and allow to rest for 5–10 minutes.

While the duck is resting, make the sauce. Combine the chilli, mint, olive oil, lemon juice and honey (or rice malt syrup, if using) with a pinch of salt and some pepper. Mix together well, taste and adjust seasoning if required.

Once the duck has rested, slice each breast on an angle. Place on a serving platter and drizzle with the sauce.

SERVES 4

CHICKEN & LEEK PIE

NUT-FREE | SUGAR-FREE | 2130 KJ/509 CAL PER SERVE

3 tablespoons butter

2 leeks, washed and thinly sliced

1 celery stick, thinly sliced

2 tablespoons plain (all-purpose) flour

250 ml (9 fl oz/1 cup) chicken stock

200 g (7 oz) button mushrooms

1 medium baked chicken, skin removed and meat shredded (it's totally okay to use a ready-cooked barbecue chicken)

2 tablespoons chopped flat-leaf (Italian) parsley

half a 375 g (13 oz) packet filo pastry

1 tablespoon butter, melted, for brushing the filo pastry

1 egg (free-range, organic), lightly beaten

Melt 2 tablespoons of the butter in a saucepan over medium heat. Add the leek and celery, stirring until they just begin to soften. Add the flour and cook, stirring, for 2 minutes. Add the chicken stock and stir until the mixture thickens.

In a frying pan, melt the remaining tablespoon of butter and cook the mushrooms until golden. Add the shredded chicken, the leek mixture and the parsley and season with salt and pepper. Allow to cool.

Meanwhile, preheat the oven to 180°C (350°F), then line a 10 × 18 cm (4 × 7 inch) pie dish with half of the sheets of filo pastry, brushing every few sheets with melted butter. Fill with the chicken mixture.

Lay the remaining sheets of pastry over the filling and tuck the edges into the pie dish to seal. Brush the top of the pie with beaten egg.

Bake for 45–50 minutes or until golden. Remove from the oven and stand for 5 minutes before serving.

SERVES 6

SALT & PEPPER PRAWNS

DAIRY-FREE | GLUTEN-FREE | NUT-FREE | PALEO | SUGAR-FREE | 1481 KJ/354 CAL PER SERVE

2 teaspoons Szechuan pepper (available from specialty delis and Asian grocers)

1 teaspoon black peppercorns

1 tablespoon sea salt flakes

small pinch of dried chilli flakes (optional)

12 raw large king prawns (shrimp), peeled and deveined, leaving tails intact

60 ml (2 fl oz/¼ cup) olive oil

lemon wedges, to serve

Soak 12 bamboo skewers in water for 30 minutes to prevent burning.

To make the spice mix, toast the Szechuan pepper and black peppercorns in a frying pan over medium–high heat until fragrant. Remove from the heat and use a mortar and pestle to grind the toasted pepper together with the sea salt flakes and chilli flakes (if using) until you have a fine powder.

Thread a skewer along the body of each prawn and sprinkle with the salt and pepper mixture.

Heat a barbecue or chargrill to medium, brushing first with the olive oil. Cook prawns for a minute each side (until they turn pink).

Serve immediately with lemon wedges.

SERVES 2

SEARED STEAK WITH CHIMICHURRI

DAIRY-FREE | GLUTEN-FREE | NUT-FREE | PALEO | 2033 KJ/486 CAL PER SERVE

1 tablespoon olive oil, plus extra for grilling

2 × 125 g (4½ oz) beef tenderloin, scotch fillet or rump steaks

Steak rub

½ tablespoon coconut or brown sugar

2 teaspoons chilli powder

¾ teaspoon ground cumin

½ teaspoon ground coriander

¾ teaspoon dried oregano

2 garlic cloves, finely chopped

Chimichurri

10 g (⅜ oz/½ cup) flat-leaf (Italian) parsley leaves

15 g (½ oz/½ cup) coriander (cilantro) leaves

1 tablespoon fresh oregano leaves

½ teaspoon dried red chilli flakes (or more, to taste)

2 garlic cloves, crushed

1 spring onion (scallion), chopped

1 tablespoon red wine vinegar

2 tablespoons olive oil

pinch of pink or white sea salt flakes

pinch of coarsely ground black pepper

Heat an oiled barbecue or chargrill to high.

Combine the ingredients for the steak rub in a bowl and mix with a fork. Season with sea salt and freshly ground black pepper to taste. Drizzle the olive oil over the steak. Coat with the rub and ensure the steak is well covered on both sides.

Cook the steak on the grill, covered with the lid or a piece of foil. Cook for about 4 minutes each side. Remove from the grill and set aside, covered, to rest.

Make the chimichurri by putting all of the dry ingredients plus the garlic and spring onion into a food processor. Pulse a few times until well chopped, but not puréed. Transfer to a bowl and add the red wine vinegar and olive oil. Whisk with a fork to combine. Season to taste with the salt and pepper.

If you don't have a food processor, finely chop all of the ingredients before mixing with the vinegar and oil.

Serve the steak with the chimichurri sauce and enjoy. Any leftover chimichurri can be kept in the fridge for a couple of days.

SERVES 2

eat well

laugh often

be thankful, always

and love

#TheGoodLife

15-MINUTE PRAWN CURRY

GLUTEN-FREE | NUT-FREE | SUGAR-FREE | 1615 KJ/386 CAL PER SERVE

2 tablespoons olive oil

4 garlic cloves, minced (enough for 2 tablespoons)

500 g (1 lb 2 oz) peeled and deveined raw prawns (shrimp)

1 large onion, thinly sliced

130 g (4½ oz/½ cup) Patak's Balti Spice Paste or similar

4 tomatoes, roughly chopped (reserve a small amount, for serving)

125 g (4½ oz/½ cup) Greek-style yoghurt

1 tablespoon cornflour (cornstarch)

100 g (3½ oz/2¼ cups) baby spinach leaves

1 tablespoon fresh coriander (cilantro) leaves, to serve

Heat 1 tablespoon of the olive oil in a large frying pan over medium–high heat. Add the garlic and stir until it is a light golden colour. Add the prawns and cook until they turn pink. Remove from the heat and transfer the prawns to a plate.

Heat the remaining olive oil in the same pan and add the onion. Cook until softened. Add the curry paste and cook for 2 minutes, stirring frequently. Add 375 ml (13 fl oz/1½ cups) of water and the tomato to the pan, mix until well combined and cook for 5 minutes, then reduce the heat to low.

In a bowl, combine the yoghurt and cornflour. Whisk with a fork until smooth and then add to the pan, stirring well until the mixture has thickened. Add the spinach. Once it is wilted, return the prawns to the pan and stir.

Transfer the curry to a serving bowl and sprinkle with the fresh coriander.

Serve immediately.

SERVES 4

STICKY LAMB RIBS

DAIRY-FREE | GLUTEN-FREE | NUT-FREE | SUGAR-FREE | 2360 KJ/564 CAL PER SERVE

2 garlic cloves, minced

90 g (3¼ oz/⅓ cup) tomato sauce (ketchup)

90 g (3¼ oz/¼ cup) honey or rice malt syrup

2 tablespoons brown sugar or stevia

2 tablespoons soy sauce or tamari

2 tablespoons brown malt vinegar

1 teaspoon dijon mustard

1.6 kg (3 lb 5 oz) lamb ribs (or you can use pork ribs)

In a large bowl, combine all of the ingredients except for the lamb ribs. Mix well. Add the ribs and gently rub the marinade all over, ensuring that all of the ribs are well coated.

Cover and refrigerate for 2 hours or, ideally, overnight.

Preheat the oven to 180°C (350°F). Line a baking tray with baking paper.

Lay the ribs on the tray and roast for approximately 1 hour, turning the ribs halfway through cooking. Serve immediately.

SERVES 4

Tip If you have time, these ribs are delicious slow cooked. Marinate as above, then cook in a slow cooker for 7–8 hours.

SEARED BEEF CARPACCIO WITH OLIVE & TOMATO TAPENADE

GLUTEN-FREE | NUT-FREE | SUGAR-FREE | 1293 KJ/309 CAL PER SERVE

500 g (1 lb 2 oz) aged eye fillet (purchase from a good butcher: ask about well-aged beef, to ensure that it's very tender)

pink salt or sea salt flakes and freshly ground black pepper

small handful of mache (corn salad) leaves, to serve

bread, to serve

Tapenade

75 g (2¾ oz/½ cup) large pitted kalamata olives, roughly chopped

500 g (1 lb 2 oz/2 punnets) sweet cherry tomatoes, quartered

250 g (9 oz/1 punnet) golden yellow cherry tomatoes, quartered

1 tablespoon baby capers, rinsed and drained

25 g (1 oz/¼ cup) grated parmesan cheese

2 tablespoons olive oil

Start by making the tapenade. Put the olives, tomatoes, capers, parmesan and olive oil in a bowl and combine well. Set aside.

Heat a frying pan over high heat. Season the beef with salt and pepper on all sides. Sear for no more than a minute, turning quickly and ensuring that all sides have been seared. Be careful not to leave the beef in the pan for any longer than is needed. Transfer to a plate or cutting board and allow to rest for a couple of minutes.

Cut the beef into very thin slices, just a few millimetres (¹⁄₁₆ inch) in thickness. Arrange the beef slices on a platter and scatter the mache leaves over. Serve with the tapenade and bread.

SERVES 4

HONEY-GLAZED SALMON

GLUTEN-FREE | NUT-FREE | SUGAR-FREE | 4753 KJ/1136 CAL PER SERVE

5 tablespoons olive oil

50 g (1¾ oz/½ cup) pearl (Israeli) couscous

250 ml (9 fl oz/1 cup) boiling water

2 salmon fillets

5 tablespoons honey or rice malt syrup

50 g (6 oz/1¾ cups) firmly packed baby kale

2 radishes, thinly sliced

150 g (5½ oz/2 cups) shredded red cabbage

14 g (½ oz/¼ cup) coriander (cilantro) leaves, roughly chopped

14 g (½ oz/¼ cup) basil leaves, roughly chopped

3 teaspoons lemon juice

1 teaspoon cayenne pepper (or more, to taste)

130 g (4½ oz/½ cup) plain yoghurt, to serve

Heat 1 tablespoon of the olive oil in a saucepan over medium heat. Add the pearl couscous and stir well, sautéing for about 1 minute. Add the boiling water to the pan, cover and reduce the heat to medium–low. Cook for about 8 minutes or until the couscous is al dente. Drain and set aside to cool.

While the couscous is cooking, coat the salmon on both sides with 2 tablespoons of the olive oil and 4 tablespoons of the honey (or rice malt syrup, if using), and season with salt and pepper.

Heat 1 tablespoon of the olive oil in a frying pan over medium–high heat. Put the salmon in the pan, skin side down, and reduce the heat to medium–low. Allow to cook for 6 minutes or until the skin is browned and crispy and the flesh begins to look opaque.

Turn the salmon over and cook for a further 2–3 minutes. Remove from the heat and set aside.

In a large bowl, combine the couscous and baby kale, radish, cabbage, coriander and basil. In a small bowl, combine the remaining olive oil, honey (or rice malt syrup), 2 teaspoons of the lemon juice, cayenne pepper and salt (to taste). Whisk together, taste and adjust seasoning if required.

In another small bowl, mix together the yoghurt and remaining lemon juice.

Dress the salad, divide between two plates and serve the salmon with a dollop of yoghurt on top.

SERVES 2

LEMON & HERB ROAST CHICKEN

DAIRY-FREE | GLUTEN-FREE | NUT-FREE | SUGAR-FREE | 2230 KJ/533 CAL PER SERVE

1 whole medium free-range (preferably organic) chicken

60 ml (2 fl oz / ¼ cup) olive oil, plus 1 tablespoon extra

1 bunch oregano

1 bunch thyme

6 garlic cloves, unpeeled

3 lemons

8 chat potatoes, halved

2 large carrots, unpeeled and roughly chopped

1 large brown or red (Spanish) onion, peeled and roughly chopped

150 g (5½ oz) mixed salad leaves, to serve

Preheat the oven to 200°C (400°F). Drizzle the chicken with olive oil and season with salt and pepper. Fill the cavity with the oregano and thyme, sliding a few sprigs of each underneath the skin. Slightly crush 2 cloves of garlic and place in the cavity.

Prick 1 lemon in several places with a knife. Put the lemon in a microwave-safe bowl and microwave for 30 seconds to release some of the juices. Place the lemon inside the chicken cavity.

Bring a medium saucepan of water to the boil over high heat. Add the potatoes and parboil for about 6 minutes. Remove from the heat and drain. Put the carrot and onion in a baking dish with the remaining 4 cloves of garlic.

Give the saucepan of potatoes a shake, just to break the potato skin a little. Add the potatoes to the baking dish. Drizzle with olive oil and season well, tossing to ensure they're all coated.

Halve the remaining lemons and slice the pointed ends off each half. Stand the lemons, widest side up, in the corners of the baking dish. Put the chicken on top of the vegies and place the baking dish in the oven. Cook for about 1 hour and 20 minutes.

Check on the chicken during cooking. At about the halfway mark, baste the vegies with the pan juices.

Once the chicken is cooked, remove it from the oven and transfer to a platter to rest, covered, for about 10 minutes. If you like your potatoes extra crispy and your onion and garlic extra caramelised, then leave them in the baking dish in the oven while the chicken is resting.

Serve the chicken and vegies with a side of mixed salad leaves, drizzled with a little olive oil.

SERVES 4 TO 6

tip Before boiling the potatoes, add a large pinch of salt to the water to speed up the boiling process.

FAB FISH FAJITAS

NUT-FREE | SUGAR-FREE | 2197 KJ/525 CAL PER SERVE

500 g (1 lb 2 oz) boneless, skinless white fish fillets, sliced into strips

2 teaspoons smoked paprika

1 teaspoon chilli powder

2 teaspoons ground cumin

1 garlic clove, minced

2½ tablespoons olive oil

8 mini tortillas, to serve

lime wedges, to serve

Salsa

8 cherry tomatoes, quartered

1 red (Spanish) onion, finely chopped

1 tablespoon finely chopped coriander (cilantro) leaves

juice of 1 lime

1 long red chilli, seeded and finely chopped

Cabbage slaw

20 g (¾ oz / ¼ cup) red cabbage, finely shredded

½ small red (Spanish) onion, thinly sliced

1 tablespoon lime juice

1 tablespoon olive oil

Smoky sour cream

125 g (4½ oz / ½ cup) light sour cream

1 teaspoon lime juice

½ teaspoon smoked paprika

pinch of salt

Coat the fish fillets with the paprika, chilli powder, cumin, garlic and olive oil, and season with salt and freshly ground black pepper. Ensure the fish is well coated.

Make the salsa by combining all of the ingredients in a bowl and seasoning with salt and freshly ground black pepper.

Make the cabbage slaw by combining all the ingredients in a bowl and seasoning with sea salt and freshly ground black pepper.

Heat a barbecue or chargrill and cook the fish for about 3–4 minutes on each side or until just cooked through. Set aside.

Make the smoky sour cream by combining all of the ingredients in a small serving bowl.

Heat the tortillas according to the packet instructions and serve with the fish, salsa, slaw, sour cream and lime wedges.

SERVES 4

tip You can use mahi mahi, blue-eye trevalla or ling for this recipe.

CHICKPEA & VEGIE CURRY

DAIRY-FREE | SUGAR-FREE | 1954 KJ/467 CAL PER SERVE

25 g (1 oz/¼ cup) flaked almonds

2 tablespoons olive oil

2 brown onions, chopped

2 garlic cloves, minced

1 teaspoon grated ginger

2 tablespoons of your favourite curry paste

400 g (14 oz) tin chopped tomatoes

2 tablespoons lime juice

400 g (14 oz) tin chickpeas, drained and rinsed

1 large zucchini (courgette), sliced into 1 cm (³/₈ inch) slices

60 g (2 oz/1 cup) broccoli florets

270 ml (9½ fl oz) tin coconut milk

140 g (5 oz/3 cups) baby spinach leaves

small handful of fresh coriander (cilantro) leaves

370 g (13 oz/2 cups) basmati rice, to serve

yoghurt (optional), to serve

Heat a small frying pan over medium heat and toast the flaked almonds for a minute or two, shaking the pan around until they turn a golden-brown colour. Remove from the heat and transfer to a bowl.

Heat the olive oil in a saucepan over medium heat. Add the onion, garlic, ginger and curry paste, stirring regularly for a few minutes. Stir in the tomatoes with a pinch of salt, and simmer until the sauce begins to thicken. Add ½ cup of cold water, the lime juice, chickpeas, zucchini and broccoli.

Cover the saucepan and cook for 15–20 minutes, stirring regularly. When the vegetables have cooked through, add the coconut milk and stir again. Reduce the heat to medium–low and simmer for another 5 minutes.

Add the spinach to the pan for the last few minutes of cooking. Taste and adjust the seasoning with salt and freshly ground black pepper if required.

Remove from the heat and allow to stand for a few minutes.

Scatter the almonds and coriander over the top and serve with the basmati rice and a dollop of yoghurt (if using).

SERVES 4

STICKY SALMON WITH RIBBON SALAD

DAIRY-FREE | GLUTEN-FREE | NUT-FREE | PALEO | SUGAR-FREE | 2088 KJ/499 CAL PER SERVE

4 salmon fillets, skin on

1 tablespoon olive oil

Marinade

1 long red chilli, seeded and finely chopped

1 garlic clove, minced

1 tablespoon olive oil

1 tablespoon lemon zest

2 tablespoons honey or rice malt syrup

1 tablespoon fish sauce

1 tablespoon sesame seeds

Ribbon salad

1 tablespoon honey or rice malt syrup

2 tablespoons rice vinegar

2 tablespoons coriander (cilantro) leaves

2 medium zucchini (courgettes), sliced into ribbons using a peeler

Combine all of the marinade ingredients except the sesame seeds in a bowl and mix well. Season with salt and pepper. Add the salmon and ensure it is well coated with the marinade. Transfer the salmon to a tray and sprinkle the sesame seeds on the skin. Cover and refrigerate for at least an hour, or preferably overnight.

Heat the olive oil in a pan over low heat. Pat the salmon gently with a paper towel and fry the salmon, skin side down for about 4–5 minutes on each side or until it is just cooked.

While the salmon is cooking, combine the honey (or rice malt syrup, if using), rice vinegar and coriander for the salad in a bowl. Add the zucchini ribbons and toss together. Serve the grilled salmon with the ribbon salad and enjoy.

SERVES 4

JAMAICAN ME CRAZY CHICKEN

DAIRY-FREE | GLUTEN-FREE | NUT-FREE | PALEO | 2770 KJ/662 CAL PER SERVE

1 brown onion, chopped

4 garlic cloves, finely chopped

2–3 habañero chillies

8 spring onions (scallions), chopped

2 tablespoons fresh thyme leaves

¾ teaspoon ground ginger

2 teaspoons ground cinnamon

½ teaspoon ground nutmeg

1½ tablespoons ground allspice

2 tablespoons coconut or brown sugar

2 tablespoons honey or rice malt syrup

60 ml (2 fl oz/¼ cup) olive oil

3 teaspoons ground black pepper

2 tablespoons pink salt flakes (or sea salt flakes)

60 ml (2 fl oz/¼ cup) lime juice (approximately 2 limes)

60 ml (2 fl oz/¼ cup) rice wine vinegar

4 free-range (preferably organic) small chicken Maryland (leg quarters), skin on

Put all of the ingredients except for the chicken into a food processor or blender, season with salt and pepper, and pulse until it becomes a paste.

Score the chicken with a sharp knife. Put the chicken in a bowl and rub the marinade all over the chicken, ensuring the marinade is inside the slits and under the skin. Cover and refrigerate overnight.

Preheat the oven to 180°C (350°F).

Remove the chicken from the fridge and lay the pieces in a large, lightly greased baking tray. Roast the chicken for approximately 50 minutes. Serve immediately.

SERVES 4

tips
- Habañero chillies are extremely hot. Use gloves when handling them (including when marinating the chicken) and be careful not to touch your eyes if you come into contact with them.
- If you can't source habañero chillies, you can use small red (bird's eye) chillies instead, however you will need around 12–16 of these in order to get the heat into the marinade.

SPICY BROCCOLI SOUP

DAIRY-FREE | NUT-FREE | PALEO | SUGAR-FREE | VEGAN | 1188 KJ/284 CAL PER SERVE

2 tablespoons olive oil

2 garlic cloves, minced

1 brown onion, diced

1 small bird's eye chilli, seeded and chopped

750 ml (26 fl oz/3 cups) vegetable stock

500 g (1 lb 2 oz) broccoli, chopped

toasted bread, to serve (optional)

Heat the olive oil in a saucepan over medium heat. Add the garlic, onion and chilli and stir until the onion has softened and the garlic has developed a golden colour. Add the stock to the saucepan, cover and increase the heat to medium–high. Once the stock is boiling, add the broccoli.

Reduce the heat to medium and simmer for about 15 minutes, stirring occasionally, until the broccoli is tender.

Remove the soup from the stovetop. Use a blender or food processor to purée the soup until smooth (or until it reaches the desired consistency). Return to the stove and warm through before serving with toasted bread (if desired).

SERVES 2

SLOW-COOKED PORK BURRITOS WITH CORN SALSA

NUT-FREE | SUGAR-FREE | 2439 KJ/583 CAL PER SERVE

1 kg (2 lb 4 oz) boneless pork shoulder, excess fat trimmed

8 flour or corn tortillas

85 g (3 oz/⅓ cup) sour cream, to serve

lime wedges, to serve

Spice rub

1 tablespoon dried oregano

2 teaspoons ground cumin

1 teaspoon ground allspice

2 teaspoons garlic powder

1 teaspoon onion powder

1 tablespoon olive oil

juice of 2 oranges, approximately 80 ml (2½ fl oz/⅓ cup)

Corn salsa

3 corncobs

½ small red (Spanish) onion, finely diced

75 g (2¾ oz/1 cup) shredded red cabbage

2 long green chillies, seeded and finely chopped

small handful of coriander (cilantro) leaves, chopped

juice of 1 lime

In a bowl, mix together the dry ingredients for the spice rub with the olive oil and half the orange juice. Put the pork in an ovenproof roasting dish and rub in the spice rub well, all over the pork. Leave to marinate for 4 hours or overnight.

Preheat the oven to 160°C (315°F). Pour the remaining orange juice gently over the top of the pork and roast the pork for 3–4 hours, spooning the pan juices over the pork every 30–40 minutes. Top up the pan with 80 ml (2½ fl oz/⅓ cup) of water if you see that the pan juices have evaporated (there should be juice in the pan at all times).

The meat is cooked when it's tender and comes apart easily.

While the pork is cooking, start on the corn salsa. Fill a large saucepan with salted water and bring to the boil. Cook the corncobs for 5 minutes, then drain.

Transfer the corn to a frying pan over medium–high heat, turning the cobs frequently until they begin to blacken. Remove from the heat and leave to cool slightly, then use a sharp knife to carefully slice off the corn kernels. Put the corn kernels into a serving bowl. Add the onion, cabbage, chilli, coriander, lime juice and sea salt to taste. Taste and adjust seasoning if required.

When the pork is ready for serving, use 2 forks to pull the meat apart and shred it in the pan. You want the pork to soak up the juices in the bottom of the pan.

Heat the tortillas according to the packet instructions.

Serve the pork with the corn salsa, sour cream, tortillas and lime wedges.

SERVES 6

ONE-POT GREEK LEMON CHICKEN & RICE

GLUTEN-FREE | NUT-FREE | SUGAR-FREE | 3837 KJ/917 CAL PER SERVE

4 small free-range (preferably organic) chicken Maryland (leg quarters), skin on

4 tablespoons olive oil, reserve half for frying

zest and juice of 2 lemons

2 garlic cloves, minced

2 large brown onions, finely diced

2 tablespoons dried oregano

2 tablespoons dried thyme

2 teaspoons sea salt

1 lemon, sliced into 1 cm (3/8 inch) thick slices

handful of flat-leaf (Italian) parsley leaves, to serve

Rice

2 tablespoons olive oil

2 large brown onions, diced

200 g (7 oz/1 cup) long-grain or medium-grain rice

1 litre (34 fl oz/4 cups) chicken stock

2 tablespoons dried oregano

2 tablespoons dried thyme

juice of one lemon

zest of one lemon, plus extra to serve

8 green (Sicilian) olives

Score the chicken and place in a bowl with 2 tablespoons of the olive oil, the zest of 2 lemons, juice of 2 lemons, garlic, onion, oregano, thyme and sea salt. Combine well, ensuring that the chicken is well coated and the marinade rubbed into the slits. Cover and refrigerate for at least an hour, preferably overnight.

Remove the chicken from the fridge. Preheat the oven to 200°C (400°F).

Heat the remaining 2 tablespoons of oil in a flameproof casserole dish or large ovenproof frying pan over medium–high heat. Put the marinade and chicken in the pan, skin side down. Sear the skin until golden brown in colour, about 5 minutes, and then turn over and repeat on the other side. Remove the chicken and onion marinade from the pan and set aside.

Return the pan to the stovetop to make the rice. Heat the olive oil. Add the onion, stirring until soft and golden. Add the rice, chicken stock, 125 ml (4 fl oz/½ cup) water, oregano, thyme, lemon juice, lemon zest and olives.

Once the stock begins to simmer, add the chicken and remove the pan from the stovetop. Cover the pan and transfer it to the oven, reducing the heat to 180°C (350°F). Bake for 30–40 minutes, adding in the lemon slices for the last 10 minutes of cooking.

When the liquid is absorbed, remove from the oven, fluff the rice with a fork and serve in the pan. Sprinkle with the remaining lemon zest and the parsley leaves before serving.

SERVES 4

salads & sides

SUPER GREEN SLAW

DAIRY-FREE | GLUTEN-FREE | NUT-FREE | PALEO | SUGAR-FREE | VEGAN | 628 KJ/150 CAL PER SERVE

550 g (1 lb 4 oz/1 bunch) baby bok choy (pak choy), washed and thinly sliced

105 g (3½ oz/1½ cups) shredded red cabbage

1 large carrot, julienned

½ red (Spanish) onion, sliced

1 small red apple, sliced into wedges

1½ tablespoons olive oil

¼ cup lemon juice

2½ teaspoons rice malt syrup

1 teaspoon dijon mustard

½ teaspoon grated ginger

In a large bowl, mix together the bok choy, cabbage, carrot, onion and apple. Set aside.

In a small bowl, whisk together the olive oil, lemon juice, rice malt syrup, mustard and ginger, then season with salt and pepper. Taste and adjust seasoning if required.

Pour the dressing over the salad and toss together well.

SERVES 4

CAULIFLOWER RICE

DAIRY-FREE | GLUTEN-FREE | NUT-FREE | PALEO | SUGAR-FREE | VEGAN | 439 KJ/105 CAL PER SERVE

750 g (26½ oz) cauliflower, roughly chopped

1 tablespoon coconut oil

1 brown onion, diced

2 garlic cloves, crushed

½ teaspoon chilli powder (or more, to taste)

small handful of coriander (cilantro) leaves, chopped

small handful of flat-leaf (Italian) parsley, chopped

3 spring onions (scallions), sliced

Pulse the cauliflower in a food processor until it looks like 'rice'. Alternatively, you can also grate the cauliflower if you don't have a food processor.

Heat the coconut oil in a frying pan over medium heat. Add the onion and garlic, stirring until softened and fragrant. Add the cauliflower and season with salt, pepper and chilli powder (if using). Add 60 ml (2 oz/¼ cup) of water and cover.

Cook, stirring occasionally, for 8–10 minutes or until the cauliflower is tender.

Remove from the heat and, while still warm, toss with the chopped herbs and spring onion.

SERVES 6

RAINBOW TOMATO SALAD WITH BURRATA

NUT-FREE | SUGAR-FREE | VEGETARIAN | 2946 KJ/704 CAL PER SERVE WITH THE DRESSING; 2234 KJ/534 CAL WITHOUT

400 g (14 oz) cherry tomato medley

250 g (9 oz/1 punnet) cherry tomatoes

2 tablespoons olive oil (optional)

2 x 200 g (7 oz) balls of burrata cheese

8 basil leaves

4 slices sourdough bread, to serve

Garlic dressing (optional)

2 garlic cloves, crushed

2 teaspoons dijon mustard

80 ml (2½ fl oz/⅓ cup) olive oil

2 teaspoons balsamic vinegar

zest of ¼ lemon

Without the garlic dressing

Cut the tomatoes into halves or quarters, put them in a bowl and add one tablespoon of the olive oil, then season with sea salt and freshly ground pepper. Toss to combine.

Arrange the tomatoes on a serving platter and top with the burrata. Drizzle with the remaining olive oil, sprinkle with basil leaves and serve with crusty bread.

With garlic dressing

Cut the tomatoes into halves or quarters, and put them in a bowl.

In a separate bowl, whisk together the dressing ingredients then season with sea salt and freshly ground pepper. Add to the tomatoes, tossing to combine.

Arrange the dressed tomatoes on a serving platter and top with the burrata. Sprinkle with basil leaves and serve with crusty bread.

SERVES 4

tip Burrata is often sold in 200 g tubs with one burrata ball per tub. Or you can buy burrata from delis.

EDAMAME & AVOCADO DIP

DAIRY-FREE | GLUTEN-FREE | NUT-FREE | PALEO | SUGAR-FREE | VEGAN | 711 KJ/170 CAL PER SERVE

90 g (3¼ oz/1½ cups) shelled edamame (available from some supermarkets, natural food markets or specialty grocers)

1 avocado, peeled, stone removed, flesh roughly chopped

¼ red (Spanish) onion, chopped

1 tablespoon lime zest

2 tablespoons lime juice, plus extra if needed

1 garlic clove, crushed

1 teaspoon grated ginger

1 tablespoon olive oil

1 teaspoon wasabi paste (or ½ small red chilli), plus extra if needed

1 tablespoon water, plus extra if needed

Combine all of the ingredients in a food processor or blender and process until smooth. Taste and adjust with extra water, lime juice, sea salt, freshly ground black pepper or wasabi.

Serve with your favourite crackers.

SERVES 4

GRAPEFRUIT & ROCKET SALAD

DAIRY-FREE | GLUTEN-FREE | NUT-FREE | PALEO | SUGAR-FREE | VEGAN | 812 KJ/194 CAL PER SERVE

1 ruby red grapefruit

1 yellow grapefruit

100 g (3½ oz) rocket (arugula)

½ small fennel bulb, thinly sliced

15 g (½ oz/¼ cup) of mizuna

15 g (½ oz/¼ cup) dill, roughly chopped

½ small red (Spanish) onion, thinly sliced

1 small avocado, peeled, stone removed, sliced

35 g (1¼ oz/¼ cup) chopped pistachio nuts (optional)

Dressing

2 tablespoons olive oil

1½ tablespoons red wine vinegar

½ teaspoon dijon mustard

Carefully peel and segment the grapefruit, removing any remaining membrane.

In a large serving bowl, gently mix together the rocket, fennel, mizuna, dill, onion, avocado and grapefruit segments.

Make the dressing by whisking together the olive oil, red wine vinegar and mustard, seasoning with salt and freshly ground black pepper.

Drizzle the salad with the dressing and top with the chopped pistachios.

SERVES 4

CHILLI BAKED RICOTTA

NUT-FREE | SUGAR-FREE | VEGETARIAN | 1339 KJ/320 CAL PER SERVE

1 kg (2 lb 4 oz) ricotta cheese, ideally in a basket

2 tablespoons olive oil

zest of ½ lemon (optional)

1 tablespoon dried chilli flakes (depending on how spicy you like it)

fresh oregano leaves, to serve

3 small pitta bread, toasted, to serve

Preheat the oven to 180°C (350°F). Line a baking tray with baking paper.

Put the ricotta on the prepared tray. Drizzle with the olive oil and sprinkle with lemon zest (if using), chilli flakes and freshly ground black pepper.

Bake for 25–30 minutes until warmed through.

Remove from the oven and finish under a hot grill (broiler) until browned at the edges.

Sprinkle with oregano. Serve with crackers or pitta bread that has been toasted under a hot grill (recommended).

SERVES 6

FIG & BUFFALO MOZZARELLA SALAD

GLUTEN-FREE | NUT-FREE | SUGAR-FREE | VEGETARIAN | 1322 KJ/316 CAL PER SERVE

2 x 110 g (4 oz) buffalo mozzarella balls

8 ripe figs

2 tablespoons olive oil

2 tablespoons caramelised balsamic vinegar (from delis or specialty food stores)

handful of basil leaves

Tear the mozzarella into thick pieces and arrange on a serving platter. Slice the figs and arrange on the platter with the mozzarella.

Drizzle the olive oil and balsamic vinegar over the figs and mozzarella.

Season with sea salt and cracked black pepper. Scatter the basil leaves over the top.

SERVES 4

SMASHED PEAS WITH BURRATA

GLUTEN-FREE | NUT-FREE | SUGAR-FREE | VEGETARIAN | 4489 KJ/1073 CAL PER SERVE

430 g (15 oz/3 cups) frozen peas

4 tablespoons olive oil

2 tablespoons lemon juice

1 garlic clove, crushed

handful of mint leaves, coarsely chopped

4 x 200 g (7 oz) balls of burrata cheese

crusty baguettes, to serve (optional)

Blanch the peas in boiling water for 2 minutes before draining.

Using a food processor or blender, combine the peas with 3 tablespoons of the olive oil, lemon juice, garlic and mint, then season with salt and freshly ground black pepper. Blend to a chunky consistency (you don't want it to be too smooth). Taste and adjust seasoning if required. If you don't have a food processor, combine the ingredients in a bowl and mash them together well using a fork.

Divide the pea mixture between 4 plates and top each with a ball of the burrata. Drizzle with the remaining olive oil. Serve with crusty bread and enjoy.

SERVES 8

Tip

Burrata is often sold in 200 g tubs with one burrata ball per tub. Or you can buy burrata from delis.

celebrate with food

nurture those you love

nourish from within

#TheGoodLife

FETA SALAD 3 WAYS

GF | NF | SF | V
908 KJ/217 CAL PER SERVE

WATERMELON & FETA SALAD

2 Lebanese (short) cucumbers, thinly sliced
100 g (3½ oz/⅔ cup) feta cheese, crumbled
½ red (Spanish) onion, thinly sliced
15 g (½ oz/¼ cup) mint leaves
2 tablespoons olive oil
¼ seedless watermelon, cut into triangles or wedges
handful of mint leaves, extra, for serving

In a large bowl, toss together the cucumber, feta, onion, mint leaves and olive oil. Arrange the watermelon on a serving platter, and sprinkle with the feta mix. Sprinkle with the extra mint leaves and serve.

SERVES 4

GF | NF | SF | V
1100 KJ/263 CAL PER SERVE

CUCUMBER & FETA SALAD WITH ZA'ATAR

200 g (7 oz/1½ cups) feta cheese, crumbled
10 g (⅜ oz/½ cup) mint leaves
60 ml (2 fl oz/¼ cup) lemon juice
2 tablespoons olive oil
4 Lebanese (short) cucumbers, thinly sliced
2 tablespoons za'atar

In a bowl, toss together the feta, mint leaves, lemon juice and olive oil. Arrange the cucumber on a serving platter and sprinkle with the feta mix. Sprinkle with the za'atar and serve.

SERVES 4

GF | NF | SF | V
1222 KJ/292 CAL PER SERVE

BEAN & FETA SALAD WITH FRESH MINT

250 g (9 oz/1⅔ cups) frozen broad beans
250 g (9 oz/1¾ cups) frozen peas
60 ml (2 fl oz/¼ cup) olive oil
1 garlic clove, crushed
2 zucchini (courgettes), sliced
zest and juice of 1 lemon
handful of mint leaves, roughly torn
100 g (3½ oz/⅔ cup) feta cheese, sliced

Bring a saucepan of water to the boil, then add the broad beans and the peas. Boil for a few minutes until tender. Drain and rinse quickly under cold water. Remove any skin from the broad beans and discard. Transfer the beans and peas to a bowl.

Heat 1 tablespoon of the olive oil in a frying pan over medium–high heat. Fry the garlic, stirring, until fragrant and golden. Add the zucchini and cook for 4–5 minutes until tender. Remove from the heat and add to the bowl with the beans and peas.

Add the lemon zest and mint leaves to the bowl and toss to combine.

Make a dressing by whisking together the lemon juice and remaining olive oil. Season with freshly ground pepper. Add to the bean mixture and mix well.

Top with feta and serve.

SERVES 4

BRUSSELS SPROUTS SALAD

SUGAR-FREE | 1745 KJ/417 CAL PER SERVE

35 g (1¼ oz/¼ cup) slivered almonds

2 x 125 g (4½ oz) chorizo sausages, sliced 1 cm (³/₈ inch) thick

300 g (10½ oz/3 cups) Brussels sprouts, outer leaves removed, stems trimmed, thinly sliced

2 tablespoons chopped flat-leaf (Italian) parsley

2 tablespoons dried cranberries (or raisins)

60 ml (2 fl oz/¼ cup) lemon juice

60 ml (2 fl oz/¼ cup) olive oil

25 g (¾ oz/¼ cup) shaved parmesan, to serve

½ lemon, cut into wedges, to serve

Heat a frying pan over medium–high heat. Dry fry the slivered almonds, shaking the pan regularly, until the almonds are lightly toasted and have a nice golden colour. Transfer from the pan to a small bowl.

Put the chorizo slices into the pan and reduce the heat to medium, then fry until cooked through.

Mix together the Brussels sprouts in a bowl with the slivered almonds, chorizo, parsley and cranberries (or raisins, if using).

In a separate bowl, make the dressing by whisking together the lemon juice and olive oil and seasoning with salt and pepper. Pour the dressing over the salad and toss well to combine.

Top with shaved parmesan and serve immediately with lemon wedges.

SERVES 4

KALE SALAD WITH PRESERVED LEMON

GLUTEN-FREE | NUT-FREE | PALEO | SUGAR-FREE | VEGAN | 439 KJ/105 CAL PER SERVE

100 g (3½ oz/4 cups) kale ribbons (stalks removed, leaves sliced)

½ small red onion, thinly sliced

450 g (1 lb/3 cups) cherry tomatoes, halved

1 tablespoon finely chopped preserved lemon rind

For the dressing

60 ml (2 fl oz/¼ cup) lemon juice

60 ml (2 fl oz/¼ cup) olive oil

1 garlic clove, crushed

½ teaspoon stevia

small pinch of ground cumin

small pinch of hot paprika

Toss together the kale, onion, cherry tomatoes and lemon rind in a bowl.

Make the dressing by whisking together all of the ingredients. Dress the salad and mix well, ensuring the kale is well coated. Serve and enjoy.

SERVES 6

tip Preserved lemons are available from delicatessens or specialty food stores.

ONE-POT QUINOA & KALE PILAF

GLUTEN-FREE | SUGAR-FREE | VEGETARIAN | 1619 KJ/387 CAL PER SERVE

200 g (7 oz/1 cup) quinoa

80 g (2¾ oz/4 cups) baby kale

juice and zest of 1 lemon

3 spring onions (scallions), chopped

1 tablespoon coconut oil (or olive oil)

½ tablespoon sumac

10 g (⅜ oz/½ cup) flat-leaf (Italian) parsley, chopped

40 g (1½ oz/¼ cup) toasted pine nuts

120 g (4 oz/1 cup) goat's cheese, crumbled

Rinse the quinoa well and set aside. Bring 500 ml (17 fl oz/ 2 cups) of salted water to the boil in a casserole dish. Add the quinoa and lower the heat to a simmer. Cook, covered, for around 10 minutes. Add the baby kale and continue to cook, covered, for another 5 minutes. Remove from the heat and check the quinoa and kale to ensure that the water has been fully absorbed and the quinoa is cooked.

Add half of the lemon juice and all of the zest, spring onion, coconut oil, sumac, parsley and pine nuts. Top with crumbled goat's cheese and serve immediately in the pot. Mix again at the table, so that the cheese melts and combines with the other ingredients. Drizzle with the remaining lemon juice for extra zing, if desired.

SERVES 4

tip Toasted pine nuts are available from supermarkets or nut shops: alternatively, dry toast raw pine nuts in a frying pan over high heat for a couple of minutes.

MASH 3 WAYS

GF | NF | SF | V
808 KJ/193 CAL PER SERVE

BROCCOLI & RICOTTA MASH

2 small potatoes, peeled and diced into 2 cm (¾ inch) cubes
500 g (17½ oz) broccoli, cut into small florets
2 tablespoons olive oil
2 garlic cloves, crushed
115 g (4 oz/½ cup) ricotta cheese
zest of 1 lemon
2 tablespoons lemon juice

Cook the potatoes in a saucepan of salted, boiling water for about 6–8 minutes. Add the broccoli and cook for another 6 minutes, or until both the potatoes and the broccoli are tender.

While the potatoes and broccoli are cooking, heat 1 tablespoon of olive oil in a small frying pan and cook the garlic until fragrant.

Drain the potatoes and broccoli and transfer to a blender or food processor. Add the garlic with the remaining oil, plus the ricotta, lemon zest and juice, and purée until you achieve a mash-like consistency (you don't want it to be too thin).

Taste and season with sea salt and freshly ground black pepper. Serve immediately.

SERVES 4

NF | SF
1431 KJ/342 CAL PER SERVE

SWEET POTATO & BACON MASH

2 large sweet potatoes, peeled and chopped
1 tablespoon butter
2 bacon rashers, fat trimmed
125 ml (4 fl oz/½ cup) coconut milk (carton variety)
1 tablespoon grated parmesan cheese (optional)

Bring a saucepan of salted water to the boil and add the sweet potato, cooking for 10–12 minutes or until tender.

Meanwhile, melt the butter in a frying pan and cook the bacon until very crispy. Transfer to a plate lined with paper towel, then crumble the bacon.

Drain the sweet potato and transfer it to a food processor or blender. Add the coconut milk and parmesan (if using), season with sea salt and freshly ground black pepper and purée until you achieve a mash-like consistency (you don't want it to be too thin).

Transfer to a serving dish and mix through a little of the crispy bacon, then top with the remainder of the bacon.

SERVES 4

GF | NF | SF | V
690 KJ/165 CAL PER SERVE

CAULIFLOWER & GARLIC MASH

500 g (17½ oz) cauliflower, cut into florets
1 tablespoon olive oil
2 garlic cloves, crushed
2 tablespoons butter
125 ml (4 fl oz/½ cup) milk

Bring a saucepan of salted water to the boil and add the cauliflower, cooking for 10–15 minutes or until the cauliflower is tender. Drain and set aside.

Meanwhile, heat the olive oil in a small pan and cook the garlic until fragrant.

Put the cauliflower, garlic, butter and milk into a food processor or blender. Purée until you achieve a mash-like consistency (you don't want it to be too thin). Season with sea salt and freshly ground black pepper to taste.

SERVES 4

GLAZED PUMPKIN

DAIRY-FREE | GLUTEN-FREE | NUT-FREE | PALEO | SUGAR-FREE | VEGAN | 494 KJ/118 CAL PER SERVE

250 ml (9 fl oz/1 cup) pulp-free orange juice

35 g (1¼ oz/⅓ cup grated) coconut sugar (available from health food stores)

½ teaspoon ground cinnamon

500 g (1 lb 2 oz) pumpkin (winter squash), chopped: golden nugget or butternut varieties will work

Preheat the oven to 200°C (400°F). Line a baking tray with baking paper and set aside.

Bring the orange juice to a boil in a saucepan over medium–high heat.

Reduce the heat to medium and add the coconut sugar, stirring well. Add the cinnamon and continue to stir occasionally for 10–15 minutes until the mixture has reduced by half.

On the baking tray, spread the chopped pumpkin out evenly so that there are no overlaps.

Using a pastry brush, baste all sides of the pumpkin with the orange juice mixture. Pop the tray into the oven and bake for 30–40 minutes (or until tender), continuing to baste every 10 minutes until cooked.

SERVES 4

GLAZED CARROTS

DAIRY-FREE | GLUTEN-FREE | PALEO | SUGAR-FREE | VEGETARIAN | 920 KJ/220 CAL PER SERVE

2 teaspoons butter

2 tablespoons coconut oil (olive oil is fine to use if you don't have coconut)

8 Dutch carrots, peeled, with green ends retained

8 purple carrots, peeled and halved lengthways

30 g (1 oz/¼ cup) walnuts, roughly chopped

½ teaspoon chilli powder

¼ teaspoon salt

2 tablespoons honey, or rice malt syrup

yoghurt, to serve (optional)

Preheat the oven to 190°C (375°F). Line a baking tray with baking paper and set aside.

Heat the butter and 1 tablespoon of the coconut oil in a saucepan over medium–high heat. When the butter has melted and combined with the coconut oil, add the carrots and cook, stirring occasionally, for about 10 minutes.

While the carrots are cooking, put the walnuts in a bowl with the remaining coconut oil and a pinch of salt. Toss to combine.

Next, sprinkle the chilli powder and salt over the carrots and stir again. Cover and continue to cook for a few more minutes, until the carrots have softened.

Remove from the heat and drizzle with the honey (or rice malt syrup, if using). Stir to coat the carrots. Add the walnuts and toss to combine.

Transfer the carrots to the prepared baking tray, and pop them into the oven for 3–5 minutes.

Remove from the oven, season with salt and freshly ground black pepper to taste. Transfer to a serving platter, and add a dollop of yoghurt, if using. Serve immediately.

SERVES 4

CHICKPEA & KALE SALAD

DAIRY-FREE | NUT-FREE | SUGAR-FREE | VEGETARIAN | 1678 KJ/401 CAL PER SERVE

2 × 400 g (14 oz) tins chickpeas, drained and rinsed

1 tablespoon olive oil

½ teaspoon salt

100 g (3½ oz/4 cups) kale ribbons (stalks removed, leaves sliced)

2 teaspoons smoked paprika, plus extra (optional) to serve

200 g (7 oz) baba ghanoush (ready-made is fine), to serve

Dressing

2 tablespoons lemon juice

60 ml (2 fl oz/¼ cup) olive oil

zest of ½ a lemon

2 teaspoons rice malt syrup

½ teaspoon crushed garlic

Preheat the oven to 190°C (375°F). Line a baking tray with baking paper and set aside.

Lay the chickpeas between two clean tea towels (dish towels) or paper towel to dry them out completely after rinsing. Remove the top towel and leave them to air dry for a few extra minutes. When dry, spread the chickpeas out on the baking tray, drizzle with the olive oil and sprinkle with salt. Very gently toss the chickpeas to ensure they are well coated.

Roast the chickpeas for 20–30 minutes until they become crunchy, stirring occasionally while they are roasting.

Meanwhile, make the dressing by whisking together all of the ingredients with a pinch of salt in a bowl. Put the kale ribbons in a clean bowl, add the dressing and toss well to combine, making sure that all of the kale is well coated.

Once the chickpeas have finished roasting, transfer them to a bowl and toss them with the paprika.

Transfer the kale to a serving platter, and top with the crunchy chickpeas and baba ghanoush. Serve immediately with extra baba ghanoush sprinkled with paprika on the side, if you like.

SERVES 4

CHIPS 4 WAYS

LEAN FAST

DF | GF | NF | P | SF | VG

812 KJ/194 CAL PER SERVE

SWEET POTATO CHIPS WITH CHILLI

1 sweet potato

olive oil spray

chilli powder

pinch of sea salt

Preheat the oven to 200°C (390°F).

Use a vegetable peeler or knife to thinly slice the sweet potato.

Spray potato lightly with olive oil on both sides, and sprinkle with chilli powder and sea salt.

Place on a wire rack and bake in the oven for about 10 minutes or until cooked and crispy.

SERVES 2

LEAN

DF | GF | NF | P | SF | VG

238 KJ/57 CAL PER SERVE

SALTED KALE CHIPS

100 g (3½ oz/1 bunch) kale (stalks removed, leaves roughly torn)

olive oil spray

½ teaspoon sea salt flakes (or more, to taste)

Preheat the oven to 150°C (300°F). Line a baking tray with baking paper and set aside.

Spray both sides of the kale leaves with oil, then place the leaves in a single layer on the prepared tray. Sprinkle with sea salt flakes.

Bake the chips in the oven for 10 minutes, then rotate the tray and bake for a further 10–15 minutes or until crispy. Leave the chips on the tray for 3 minutes before serving.

SERVES 2

Tip Use the kale stems in a green smoothie!

LEAN

DF | GF | NF | P | SF | VG

247 KJ/59 CAL PER SERVE

SPICY PAPRIKA KALE CHIPS

100 g (3½ oz/1 bunch) kale (stalks removed, leaves roughly torn)

olive oil spray

½ teaspoon smoked paprika

pinch of sea salt (optional)

Preheat the oven to 150°C (350°F). Line a baking tray with baking paper and set aside.

Spray both sides of the kale leaves with oil and sprinkle lightly with paprika and salt (if using).

Place the leaves on the tray in a single layer and bake in the oven for 10 minutes.

Rotate the tray and bake for a further 10–15 minutes or until crispy. Leave the chips on the tray for 3 minutes before serving.

SERVES 2

FAB

GF | NF | SF | V

1816 KJ/434 CAL PER SERVE

BAKED GARLIC & PARMESAN CHIPS

3 potatoes, washed and cut into matchsticks

1 tablespoon garlic powder

2 tablespoons olive oil

3 tablespoons grated parmesan cheese

2 teaspoons finely chopped flat-leaf (Italian) parsley

Preheat the oven to 180°C (350°F). Line a baking tray with baking paper and set aside.

Put the potato matchsticks in a large bowl and toss them together with the garlic and olive oil, then season with sea salt and freshly ground black pepper.

Arrange the matchsticks on the prepared tray in a single layer, so they don't overlap each other.

Bake the chips for 10–15 minutes, then turn them over and cook for another 10 minutes until cooked and golden.

Remove the tray from the oven and immediately sprinkle the chips with the grated parmesan so that it melts. Sprinkle the parsley over the top and serve.

SERVES 2

sauces &

sesame ponzu
dressing

orange &
poppyseed
dressing

spicy
japanese
mayo

super green
pesto

marinades

tzatziki

herb & yoghurt
dressing

harissa
paste

SUPER GREEN PESTO

(LEAN) (FAST)

DF | GF | P | SF | VG
941 KJ/225 CAL PER SERVE

60 g (2¼ oz/1 cup) broccoli florets

½ small avocado, peeled, stone removed

50 g (1¾ oz/2 cups) kale ribbons (stalks removed, leaves sliced)

2 garlic cloves, minced

40 g (1½ oz/¼ cup) pine nuts

60 g (2¼ oz/½ cup) walnuts

2 tablespoons lemon juice

30 g (1 oz/1 cup loosely packed) basil leaves (about half a bunch)

small handful of flat-leaf (Italian) parsley leaves

60 ml (2 fl oz/¼ cup) olive oil, plus extra, if needed

Put the broccoli in a blender or food processor and pulse a couple of times quickly, just to chop it into smaller pieces.

Add the remaining ingredients and blend until the pesto reaches the desired consistency, adding a little more olive oil if required. Season with sea salt and freshly ground black pepper. Store in an airtight container. It will keep in the fridge for 2–3 days.

SERVES 6

HARISSA PASTE

(LEAN) (FAST)

DF | GF | NF | P | SF | VG
402 KJ/96 CAL PER SERVE

1 teaspoon caraway seeds

5 long red chillies, seeded and chopped

3 garlic cloves, crushed

½ teaspoon salt, or more to taste

1 teaspoon ground cumin

1 teaspoon ground coriander

1 teaspoon smoked paprika

60 ml (2 fl oz/¼ cup) olive oil

Heat a frying pan over medium–high heat and dry-fry the caraway seeds, tossing a couple of times and then removing the pan from the heat. Use a mortar and pestle to crush the seeds to a powder.

Add the remaining ingredients to the mortar and pound to a fine paste. Add a little more olive oil if required.

Store in an airtight container in the fridge for up to 10 days.

SERVES 6

ORANGE & POPPYSEED DRESSING

(LEAN) (FAST)

DF | GF | NF | P | SF | V
473 KJ/113 CAL PER SERVE

2 teaspoons poppy seeds

60 ml (2 fl oz/¼ cup) orange juice

2 teaspoons orange zest

¼ teaspoon dijon mustard

3 teaspoons honey

2 tablespoons olive oil

Combine all of the ingredients in a bowl, season with salt and whisk together until well combined.

Store in an airtight container in the fridge for up to 3 days.

SERVES 4

NF | SF | V
377 KJ/90 CAL PER SERVE

HERB & YOGHURT DRESSING

1 tablespoon horseradish cream (from condiment section of supermarket)

25 g (1 oz / ½ cup firmly packed) basil leaves

15 g (½ oz / ¾ cup) flat-leaf (Italian) parsley

260 g (9¼ oz / 1 cup) Greek-style yoghurt

Put the horseradish cream, basil, parsley and ¼ cup of the yoghurt into a food processor and purée until smooth. Transfer to a bowl and stir in the remaining yoghurt.

Store in an airtight container in the fridge for up to 1 week.

SERVES 4

DF | NF | P | SF | V
531 KJ/127 CAL PER SERVE

SESAME PONZU DRESSING

2 tablespoons soy sauce

80 ml (2½ fl oz / ⅓ cup) ponzu (from Asian sauce section of your supermarket)

2 tablespoons sesame oil

1 tablespoon sesame seeds

Combine all of the ingredients in a bowl and whisk together.

Store in an airtight container in the fridge for up to 2 weeks.

SERVES 4

DF | GF | NF | P | SF | V
912 KJ/218 CAL PER SERVE

SPICY JAPANESE MAYO

120 g (4¼ oz / ½ cup) Japanese mayonnaise (such as Kewpie)

3 tablespoons sriracha (chilli sauce), or to taste

2 teaspoons lemon juice

Combine all of the ingredients in a small bowl and mix well.

Store in an airtight container in the fridge for up to 2 weeks.

SERVES 4

GF | NF | SF | V
343 KJ/82 CAL PER SERVE

TZATZIKI

260 g (9¼ oz / 1 cup) Greek-style yoghurt

zest and juice of 1 lemon

1 garlic clove, crushed

5 g (¼ cup) mint leaves, finely chopped, plus extra whole mint leaves to serve

Mix all of the ingredients together in a bowl, season with salt and top with the extra mint leaves.

Store in an airtight container in the fridge for up to 1 week.

SERVES 4

dessert

BERRYLICIOUS MERINGUE

GLUTEN-FREE | VEGETARIAN | 2669 KJ/638 CAL PER SERVE

butter, for greasing

7 large egg whites (free-range, organic)

300 g (10½ oz/1⅓ cups) sugar, or 150 g (5½ oz) stevia

80 g (2¾ oz/¾ cup) hazelnut meal

1 litre (35 fl oz/4 cups) thickened (whipping) cream

1 vanilla bean, split and seeds scraped

150 g (5½ oz) icing sugar or icing stevia

500 g (1 lb 2 oz) raspberries

500 g (1 lb 2 oz) blueberries

500 g (1 lb 2 oz) strawberries

Preheat the oven to 120°C (250°F). Lightly grease 4 baking trays, line with baking paper and lightly grease the paper.

In the bowl of an electric mixer that is fitted with the whisk attachment, beat the egg whites with the sugar until stiff, then fold the hazelnut meal into the mixture.

Divide the mixture between the 4 baking trays. We use the ring of a springform cake pan as a guide to keeping them all approximately the same size. Spread to a 1–1.5 cm (⅜–⅝ inch) thickness.

Bake for 50 minutes or until set and nearly crisp, then turn onto a wire rack and peel off the baking paper. You need to do this while the meringues are still hot.

Put the cream into a bowl, scrape the seeds from the vanilla bean into the cream, add the icing sugar and beat with electric beaters until peaks form.

Place a meringue layer on a large flat serving plate and cover with a quarter of the cream mixture. Scatter a quarter of each of the berries over the cream, then repeat with remaining meringues, cream and berries.

SERVES 10

Tips
- Add 1 teaspoon of lemon juice per egg white to help the egg whites stiffen.
- Make sure the bowls and utensils are clean.

GOOEY CHOC CARAMEL SLICE

DAIRY-FREE | GLUTEN-FREE | PALEO | SUGAR-FREE | VEGETARIAN | 1218 KJ/291 CAL PER SERVE

Chocolate

55 g (2 oz/½ cup) unsweetened cocoa powder

60 ml (2 fl oz/¼ cup) coconut oil

80 ml (2½ fl oz/⅓ cup) maple syrup

Caramel

260 g (9 oz/1 cup) almond spread

250 ml (9 fl oz/1 cup) maple syrup

1 tablespoon natural vanilla extract

½ teaspoon sea salt

170 ml (5½ fl oz/⅔ cup) coconut oil

Line a 16 cm (6¼ inch) square tin with baking paper.

To make the chocolate, combine all of the ingredients in a bowl and microwave for 15 seconds, stir thoroughly to combine and microwave again for another 15 seconds. Repeat until a smooth mixture is achieved.

Pour the chocolate into the tin and spread evenly, using a spatula or knife. Freeze for 10–15 minutes to set.

Meanwhile make the caramel by combining all of the ingredients in a saucepan over medium–low heat. Stir constantly until well combined. Remove from the heat and allow to cool.

Remove the chocolate base from the freezer and pour the cooled caramel over the top of the chocolate. Carefully smooth out the caramel with a spatula or knife to ensure it's evenly distributed. Return the tin to the freezer for 45–60 minutes to set.

When the caramel has set, carefully lift the slice out of the tin and cut it in half. Press the halves together to make a 'sandwich'. Cut into 16 pieces and store in the freezer in an airtight container until ready to serve.

MAKES 16

FRO-YO BARK 4 WAYS

GF | NF | SF | V
607 KJ/145 CAL PER SERVE

BLUEBERRY BLISS

520 g (1 lb 2½ oz/2 cups) Greek-style yoghurt

1 teaspoon natural vanilla extract

2 tablespoons honey or rice malt syrup (or you can swap for 2 teaspoons stevia)

125 g (4½ oz/1 cup) frozen blueberries

fresh blueberries (optional), to serve

In a large bowl, combine the yoghurt, vanilla and honey. Add the frozen blueberries and gently mix.

Line a tray with baking paper and spread out the yoghurt mixture, so that it's around 1 cm (³/8 inch) thick. Put the tray in the freezer for 1 hour or until the mixture is completely frozen.

Remove the tray from the freezer and use a sharp knife to break up the bark into shards. Serve with the fresh berries, if desired.

SERVES 6

GF | NF | SF | V
665 KJ/159 CAL PER SERVE

RASPBERRY COCONUT

520 g (1 lb 2½ oz/2 cups) Greek-style yoghurt, plain or coconut-flavoured

2 tablespoons honey or rice malt syrup (or you can swap for 2 teaspoons stevia)

125 g (4½ oz/1 cup) frozen raspberries

30 g (1 oz/½ cup) coconut flakes

In a large bowl, gently combine the yoghurt, honey and half the raspberries. Add the coconut flakes and gently mix.

Line a tray with baking paper and spread out the yoghurt mixture, so that it's around 1 cm (³/8 inch) thick. Top with the remaining raspberries and put the tray in the freezer for 1 hour or until the mixture is completely frozen.

Remove the tray from the freezer and use a sharp knife to break up the bark into shards.

SERVES 6

GF | SF | V
791 KJ/189 CAL PER SERVE

FRUIT & NUT

520 g (1 lb 2½ oz/2 cups) Greek-style yoghurt

2 tablespoons honey or rice malt syrup (or you can swap for 2 teaspoons stevia)

35 g (1¼ oz/¼ cup) roughly chopped hazelnuts

40 g (1½ oz/¼ cup) dried cranberries, or dried fruit of your choice

In a large bowl, combine the yoghurt and honey. Add most of the hazelnuts and cranberries and gently mix.

Line a tray with baking paper and spread out the yoghurt mixture, so that it's around 1 cm (³/8 inch) thick. Top with the remaining fruit and nuts and put the tray in the freezer for 1 hour or until the mixture is completely frozen.

Remove the tray from the freezer and use a sharp knife to break up the bark into shards.

SERVES 6

NF | SF | V
841 KJ/201 CAL PER SERVE

DARK CHOCOLATE & DATE

520 g (1 lb 2½ oz/2 cups) Greek-style yoghurt

3 fresh dates, roughly chopped

75 g (2¾ oz/½ cup) roughly chopped dark chocolate

In a large bowl, combine the yoghurt, dates and most of the chocolate and gently mix.

Line a tray with baking paper and spread out the yoghurt mixture, so that it's around 1 cm (³/8 inch) thick. Top with the remaining chocolate and put the tray in the freezer for 1 hour or until the mixture is completely frozen.

Remove the tray from the freezer and use a sharp knife to break up the bark into shards.

SERVES 6

Tips
- Leftovers can be stored in an airtight container or resealable plastic bags in the freezer for up to 10 days.
- Serve with a dusting of cocoa powder and your favourite nut butter or Nice cream (see page 233).

TAPIOCA PUDDINGS WITH COCONUT & MANGO

DAIRY-FREE | GLUTEN-FREE | NUT-FREE | VEGETARIAN | 1464 KJ/389 CAL PER SERVE

65 g (2¼ oz/⅓ cup) small tapioca pearls

250 ml (9 fl oz/1 cup) unsweetened vanilla almond milk (note: you can use any milk)

400 g (14 oz) tin coconut milk

110 g (3¾ oz/½ cup) sugar, or ½ cup stevia

1 teaspoon natural vanilla extract

1 vanilla bean, split and seeds scraped

pinch of salt

1 mango, finely diced

1 tablespoon grated lime zest

2 tablespoons lime juice

Soak the tapioca pearls in the vanilla almond milk for about an hour.

Transfer the soaked tapioca pearls and any unabsorbed milk to a saucepan and add the coconut milk, sugar, vanilla extract, vanilla bean seeds and the salt. Bring to a boil over medium heat, stirring occasionally. Reduce the heat and simmer for 20 minutes, stirring occasionally.

Remove from the heat and allow the mixture to cool.

Mix the diced mango with the lime zest and lime juice.

To serve, divide the tapioca pudding between the glasses, then top with the mango.

Cover the puddings and refrigerate for about 2 hours, or until chilled, before serving.

SERVES 4

2-MINUTE CHOCOLATE MUG CAKE

DAIRY-FREE | SUGAR-FREE | VEGETARIAN | 2209 KJ/528 CAL PER SERVE

1 tablespoon coconut oil, melted

2 tablespoons honey, or maple syrup

1 egg (free-range, organic)

2 tablespoons unsweetened almond milk

2 tablespoons plain (all-purpose) flour, or almond meal

1 tablespoon unsweetened cocoa powder, plus ½ teaspoon extra

1 vanilla bean, split and seeds scraped

In a microwave-safe mug, mix together the wet ingredients. Add the dry ingredients and mix again.

Pop the mug into the microwave for around 1–1½ minutes (depending on the power of your microwave).

Serve with a dusting of extra cocoa powder and your favourite nut spread or Nice Cream (see page 233).

SERVES 1

tip Make this mug cake immediately before serving as it's best enjoyed warm.

NICE CREAM 4 WAYS

DAIRY-FREE | GLUTEN-FREE | NUT-FREE | PALEO | SUGAR-FREE | VEGETARIAN | VEGAN

---

477 KJ/114 CAL PER SERVE

CHOCOLATE

4 ripe bananas, peeled, cut into chunks and frozen

½ teaspoon ground cinnamon

4 tablespoons unsweetened cocoa or cacao powder

1 teaspoon stevia (optional)

389 KJ/93 CAL PER SERVE

VANILLA BANANA

4 ripe bananas, peeled, cut into chunks and frozen

1 teaspoon ground cinnamon

1 tablespoon natural vanilla extract

1 vanilla bean, split and seeds scraped

523 KJ/125 CAL PER SERVE

RASPBERRY

4 ripe bananas, peeled, cut into chunks and frozen

300 g (11 oz/2½ cups) raspberries, half for blending and half to fold through before freezing

½ teaspoon stevia

519 KJ/124 CAL PER SERVE

SALTED DATE CARAMEL

4 ripe bananas, peeled, cut into chunks and frozen

10 dates, pitted (if dried, soak in warm water for 10 minutes, then drain)

1 teaspoon sea salt

2–4 tablespoons warm water (optional), for thinning

If making the salted date caramel, put the dates in a food processor or blender and purée until smooth. If necessary, add warm water to create a smooth consistency. Season with sea salt and blend once more to combine well. Set aside until you are ready to add the flavour after puréeing the frozen banana.

Put the frozen banana chunks in a food processor or upright blender and pulse. At first the banana will look crumbly, so scrape down the sides and continue processing. It will start to look a bit mushy. Don't worry! Scrape down the sides and continue processing. It will become smoother but still with a few banana chunks in it. Scrape down the sides

of the processor and continue processing. You'll see it almost magically change from mush to the consistency of soft-serve ice cream.

Now add the extra ingredients to create your chosen flavour and process once more to combine the ingredients.

Transfer to an airtight container and freeze until solid, like traditional ice cream. You can eat the ice cream immediately: it will be quite soft, but still yummy!

SERVES 4

tip Nice cream has an underlying taste of banana, because … it's banana! It's designed to be a tasty ice cream-like dessert for when you feel like a sweet treat.

RHUBARB & VANILLA PIE

NUT-FREE | VEGETARIAN | 1347 KJ/322 CAL PER SERVE

400 g (14 oz/1 bunch) rhubarb stalks, trimmed and thinly sliced

185 g (6½ oz/1 cup lightly packed) brown sugar, or healthy brown sugar alternative (see below)

1 tablespoon cornflour (cornstarch)

2 vanilla beans, split and seeds scraped

1 teaspoon lemon juice

2 sheets ready-made frozen puff pastry, thawed

1 egg white (free-range, organic), lightly beaten, for brushing

icing sugar or icing stevia, for sprinkling

Preheat the oven to 160°C (315°F).

Put the rhubarb, brown sugar, cornflour, vanilla and lemon juice in a bowl and mix well to combine. Transfer to a colander over a large bowl to drain of liquid for 2–3 hours. Discard the liquid.

Line the base of a lightly greased 22 cm (8½ inch) pie tin with one sheet of the pastry, ensuring the pastry reaches the sides of the tin. Spoon the drained rhubarb mixture onto the pastry.

Using a ravioli cutter or knife, cut another sheet of pastry into 8–12 strips, each 2 cm (¾ inch) wide. Arrange the strips on top of the pie to make a lattice pattern. Press the edges to seal and trim off the excess.

Brush with egg white and sprinkle with icing sugar or icing stevia.

Bake for 45 minutes or until the pastry is golden and crisp.

SERVES 6

HEALTHY BROWN SUGAR ALTERNATIVE

60 ml (2 fl oz/¼ cup) sugar-free maple syrup, or 1 cup stevia

¾ teaspoon molasses (blackstrap is preferred)

2–4 drops butterscotch or maple extract

Mix together and use in place of brown sugar.

NO-BAKE COCONUT BARS

DAIRY-FREE | GLUTEN-FREE | NUT-FREE | PALEO | SUGAR-FREE | VEGETARIAN | 854 KJ/204 CAL PER SERVE

130 g (4½ oz/2 cups) shredded coconut

3 tablespoons honey

3 tablespoons coconut oil

2 teaspoons vanilla bean paste

pinch of salt

juice and finely grated zest of 1 lime

75 g (2⅔ oz/½ cup) dried cranberries (optional)

Line a baking tray or loaf tin with baking paper.

Put all of the ingredients except the cranberries into a food processor and pulse to combine to a rough crumb consistency; don't overprocess. Fold in the cranberries, if using. Spread the mixture onto a baking tray or press into a loaf tin.

Chill in the freezer for 20 minutes. Cut into bars when frozen. Store, refrigerated, in an airtight container for up to a week.

MAKES 8 BARS

RAW CARAMEL APPLE PIE

DAIRY-FREE | GLUTEN-FREE | PALEO | SUGAR-FREE | VEGAN | VEGETARIAN | 1761 KJ/421 CAL PER SERVE

175 g (6 oz/1½ cups) walnuts

10 medjool dates, pitted

Filling

4 granny smith apples, peeled

1 tablespoon ground cinnamon

125 g (4½ oz) blueberries, to serve

Caramel sauce

3 medjool dates, pitted

60 ml (2 fl oz/¼ cup) maple syrup

125 ml (4 fl oz/½ cup) coconut oil

90 g (3¼ oz/⅓ cup) almond spread

1 teaspoon natural vanilla extract

¼ teaspoon salt

125 ml (4 fl oz/½ cup) water

Put the 3 dates for the caramel sauce in a small bowl and cover with hot water. Soak for 10–15 minutes.

Line the base of a 20 cm (8 inch) round tart tin with baking paper and set aside. Alternatively, use 8 ovenproof ramekins.

In a food processor, blend the walnuts into a fine meal. Add the 10 unsoaked dates and process until combined. Press the date and walnut mixture into the tart pan as the base. Cover with plastic wrap and freeze until ready to use.

To make the apple filling, peel and thinly slice the apples and coat with the cinnamon.

To make the caramel sauce, put all of the ingredients in a blender and add the 3 dates that have been soaking (discard the water). Blend until smooth. Pour the caramel sauce over the apple slices and toss until evenly coated.

Remove the pie crust from the freezer and fill with apple filling. Freeze for at least 45 minutes and thaw just before serving, then top with fresh blueberries.

The pie will keep in an airtight container in the freezer for up to 6 weeks.

SERVES 10

SUPER QUICK COCONUT CHOC

DAIRY-FREE | GLUTEN-FREE | NUT-FREE | PALEO | SUGAR-FREE | VEGAN | VEGETARIAN | 837 KJ/200 CAL PER SERVE

125 ml (4 fl oz/½ cup) coconut oil

5 tablespoons rice malt syrup

120 g (4¼ oz/½ cup) cacao or cocoa powder

100 g (3½ oz/1½ cups) shredded coconut

Melt the coconut oil in a saucepan over low heat. When melted, remove from the heat, add the rice malt syrup, whisking briskly until well combined. Add the cacao powder, stirring well until completely mixed through.

Add the shredded coconut and stir through the chocolate mixture. Spread evenly on a lined baking tray and freeze for 30–60 minutes or until set.

Cut into 12 pieces and serve immediately or store in the freezer in an airtight container.

MAKES ABOUT 12

MINTY PINK GRAPEFRUIT GRANITA

DAIRY-FREE | GLUTEN-FREE | NUT-FREE | VEGAN | VEGETARIAN | 519 KJ/124 CAL PER SERVE

300 g (10½ oz/1⅓ cups) sugar, or 100 g (3½ oz) stevia

4 large pink grapefruits, flesh scooped out, skin and pith removed

juice of 1 lime

5 g (³/₁₆ oz/¼ cup) mint leaves, shredded, plus extra for garnish

In a small saucepan, heat 300 ml (10½ fl oz/1¼ cups) of water with the sugar or stevia over medium heat, stirring often until the sugar dissolves. Remove from the heat and cool completely.

In a blender, combine the cooled syrup, pink grapefruit and the lime juice. Process on high until the mixture is well blended.

Pour the granita mix into a shallow tin. Sprinkle the shredded mint leaves over the top. Cover with plastic wrap and freeze for 4 hours. Scrape the frozen mixture with a fork, cover and return to the freezer for another 4 hours or overnight.

Serve by scraping the granita with a fork again, then spooning it into cocktail glasses. Garnish with extra mint leaves.

SERVES 12

tip If you're in a hurry, swap the grapefruit for 375–500 ml (13–17 fl oz/1½–2 cups) of store-bought grapefruit juice.

CHEESECAKE WITH BERRY COULIS

GLUTEN-FREE | NUT-FREE | VEGETARIAN | 1866 KJ/446 CAL PER SERVE

1 teaspoon butter, for greasing

690 g (1 lb 8½ oz/3 cups) ricotta, drained as long as possible (ideally overnight)

120 ml (4¼ fl oz) honey, or 200 ml (7 fl oz) rice malt syrup

2 teaspoons lemon zest

2 eggs (free-range, organic)

Berry coulis

250 g (9 oz/2 cups) frozen mixed berries

1 tablespoon sugar, or ½ teaspoon stevia (optional)

Preheat the oven to 180°C (350°F). Lightly grease 4 large ramekins.

Whisk the ricotta, honey (or rice malt syrup, if using), lemon zest and eggs in a bowl until well combined. Divide the mixture between the ramekins.

Bake for around 30 minutes or until lightly golden brown on the top.

Meanwhile, bring the berries and sugar (or stevia, if using) to the boil over medium–high heat. Remove from the heat and allow to cool.

Remove the ramekins from the oven and spoon the cooled berry coulis over the top of each one. Serve immediately.

SERVES 4

POPSICLES 2 WAYS

GF | NF | SF | V
628 KJ/150 CAL PER SERVE

RASPBERRY VANILLA POPSICLES

250 g (9 oz/2 cups) raspberries, fresh or frozen

1 teaspoon natural vanilla extract

small handful of basil leaves

520 g (1 lb 2½ oz/2 cups) vanilla Greek-style yoghurt

In a blender or food processor, purée the raspberries, vanilla and basil leaves until smooth. If you're using frozen raspberries, not fresh, you may need to add 60 ml (2 fl oz/¼ cup) of water to help with the blending.

Using popsicle (ice lolly) moulds, alternately spoon in the berry mixture and yoghurt. Freeze for about 6 hours, or ideally overnight.

MAKES 5

DF | GF | NF | P | SF | V
310 KJ/74 CAL PER SERVE

MANGO & COCONUT POPSICLES

315 g (11⅛ oz/1 cup) mango chunks, fresh or frozen

60 ml (2 fl oz/¼ cup) coconut milk (carton variety)

1 teaspoon natural vanilla extract

juice of 1 lime

20 g (¾ oz/¼ cup) shredded coconut

In a blender or food processor, purée the mango, coconut milk, vanilla and lime juice until smooth. If you're using frozen mango, not fresh, you may need to add an extra 60 ml (2 fl oz/¼ cup) of coconut milk to help with the blending.

When puréed, gently stir in the shredded coconut.

Using popsicle (ice lolly) moulds, spoon in the mango coconut mixture. Freeze for about 6 hours, or ideally overnight.

MAKES 5

INDIVIDUAL RASPBERRY & CHOCOLATE PUDDINGS

NUT-FREE | VEGETARIAN | 1615 KJ/386 CAL PER SERVE

vegetable oil, for greasing

300 g (10½ oz) raspberries

55 g (2¼ oz/¼ cup) caster (superfine) sugar or stevia

50 g (1¾ oz/⅓ cup) self-raising flour

40 g (1½ oz/¼ cup) plain (all-purpose) flour

2 tablespoons unsweetened cocoa, or raw cacao powder

2 tablespoons skim milk

1 egg (free-range, organic), whisked lightly

2 tablespoons raspberry jam, or sugar-free raspberry 'jam' (see below)

1 tablespoon vegetable oil, extra

1 teaspoon natural vanilla extract

125 ml (4 fl oz/½ cup) double cream, to serve

icing sugar, or sugar-free icing, to dust (optional)

Preheat the oven to 180°C (350°F). Brush four 125 ml (4 fl oz/ ½ cup) ovenproof dishes or ramekins with the vegetable oil to lightly grease.

Put the raspberries in a bowl and sprinkle with 1 tablespoon of the sugar (or stevia). Toss to combine, leave to sit for around 5 minutes, then spoon evenly over the bases of the greased dishes.

Sift the self-raising flour, plain flour and cocoa into a medium bowl. Add the remaining sugar, milk, egg, jam, oil and vanilla. Use an electric beater on low speed to beat until just combined.

Spoon the mixture evenly into the prepared dishes. Stand the dishes on a baking tray and bake for 25–30 minutes or until a skewer inserted in the centres of the puddings comes out clean.

Dust with icing sugar (if using) and serve immediately with cream.

SERVES 4

SUGAR-FREE RASPBERRY JAM

250 g (9 oz/2 cups) raspberries (if using frozen, defrost first)

2–3 tablespoons honey or maple syrup, or rice malt syrup

3 tablespoons chia seeds

½ teaspoon natural vanilla extract (optional)

In a medium saucepan, bring the raspberries to a low boil, stirring frequently. Reduce the heat to low and simmer for about 5 minutes or until the berries soften. Lightly mash the berries with a fork or potato masher, but leave some chunks in for texture.

Stir in the honey or maple syrup and chia seeds. Cook the jam on low for 5–7 minutes or until it thickens. Keep stirring so that it doesn't stick.

Remove from the heat and stir in the vanilla. Allow the jam to cool to room temperature. Pour into a jar or airtight container and store in the fridge. It should keep for up to 2 weeks in the fridge.

MAKES 2 CUPS

DESSERT

LEAN & LUSCIOUS YOGHURT & BERRY TART

SUGAR-FREE | VEGETARIAN | 1188 KJ/284 CAL PER SERVE

100 g (3½ oz/1 cup) pecan nuts

170 g (6 oz/1 cup) pitted dates

150 g (5½ oz/1½ cups) oats

2 tablespoons desiccated coconut

1 teaspoon ground cinnamon

3 tablespoons honey or maple syrup, or 6 tablespoons rice malt syrup

Filling

390 g (13¾ oz/1½ cups) Greek-style yoghurt

2 tablespoons honey or maple syrup, or 4 tablespoons rice malt syrup

1 teaspoon natural vanilla extract

300 g (10½ oz) fresh blueberries

Preheat the oven to 180°C (350°F). Line a 20 cm (8 inch) springform tin with baking paper.

Put the pecans, dates, oats, coconut and cinnamon into a food processor and pulse until you have a mixture with a fine grain. Add the honey and 80 ml (2½ fl oz/⅓ cup) of water and pulse until the mixture starts to stick together in a ball.

Put the mixture in the springform tin and spread it out evenly, pushing the mixture halfway up the side of the tin. Make sure it is well compacted by pushing down with the back of a spoon.

Bake for 15 minutes or until golden. Set aside to cool.

To make the filling, mix the yoghurt with the honey and vanilla. When the crust is cool, spread the yoghurt mixture into the crust and top with the blueberries.

You can serve it immediately or keep the tart, covered, in the fridge for a few days, though the crust will become more fragile because it will absorb moisture from the yoghurt; however, it will still taste great!

SERVES 10

VANILLA PANNA COTTA WITH FIGS & HONEY

GLUTEN-FREE | NUT-FREE | VEGETARIAN | 1397 KJ/334 CAL PER SERVE

250 ml (9 fl oz/1 cup) thin (pouring) cream

110 g (3¾ oz/½ cup) caster (superfine) sugar or stevia

1 vanilla bean, split and seeds scraped

2 cinnamon sticks

4 teaspoons powdered gelatine

500 ml (17 fl oz/2 cups) buttermilk

Honeyed figs

60 ml (2 fl oz/¼ cup) dry red wine

90 g (3¼ oz/¼ cup) honey, or maple syrup or rice malt syrup

3 figs, halved

Combine the cream, sugar (or stevia), vanilla seeds and cinnamon in a medium saucepan and stir over a low heat until the sugar dissolves. Bring to the boil. Strain the mixture into a large heatproof jug and allow to cool for 5 minutes.

Sprinkle the gelatine over 2 tablespoons of water in a small heatproof jug. Stand the jug in a small saucepan of simmering water and stir until the gelatine dissolves. Allow to cool for 5 minutes.

Stir the gelatine mixture and the buttermilk into the cream mixture. Divide the mixture into six 1805 ml (6 fl oz/¾ cup) panna cotta moulds. Cover and refrigerate for 4 hours or until they are set.

To make the honeyed figs, combine all of the ingredients in a medium saucepan and bring to the boil. Reduce the heat and simmer, uncovered, for about 5 minutes or until the syrup thickens slightly. Cool.

Turn the panna cottas onto serving plates, or into dessert bowls or glasses, and top with the honeyed figs.

SERVES 6

FUDGE FIX

DAIRY-FREE | GLUTEN-FREE | PALEO | SUGAR-FREE | VEGETARIAN | 1561 KJ/373 CAL PER SERVE

160 g (5¾ oz/1 cup) pitted dates

80 g (2¾ oz/½ cup) whole almonds

30 g (1 oz/¼ cup) walnuts

30 g (1 oz/¼ cup) unsweetened cocoa powder

8–10 walnuts, extra, roughly chopped, for topping

Icing

2 small ripe bananas

4 tablespoons almond spread, or nut spread of your choice

30 g (1 oz/¼ cup) unsweetened cocoa powder

4 tablespoons honey or 6 tablespoons rice malt syrup

Soak the dates in a bowl of warm water for 30 minutes, then drain, discarding the water.

Mix together the dates, almonds, walnuts and cocoa in a food processor until well combined.

Spread the mixture into a greased 20 cm (8 inch) square baking tray until evenly distributed. Use the back of a spoon or, if you find that the mixture is too sticky, lightly wet your hands.

Blend all of the ingredients for the icing in a food processor until well combined. Spread the mixture over the bottom layer until evenly distributed.

Freeze for 45 minutes or until firm. Cut into 16 squares and top with the chopped walnuts. Store in the freezer for up to 2 weeks.

MAKES 16

LAZY LEMON TART

NUT-FREE | SUGAR-FREE | VEGETARIAN | 1724 KJ/412 CAL PER SERVE

4 eggs (free-range, organic) plus 4 egg yolks

170 ml (5½ fl oz/⅔ cup) honey or 250 ml (9 fl oz/1 cup) rice malt syrup

250 ml (9 fl oz/1 cup) lemon juice

zest of 4 lemons

125 g (4½ oz/½ cup) butter or coconut oil

1 ready-made tart shell, 20 cm (8 inch) diameter

In a medium saucepan, whisk together the eggs and egg yolks, honey (or rice malt syrup, if using), lemon juice and zest, and add a generous pinch of salt. Add the butter or coconut oil and cook over medium–low heat, whisking constantly for about 8 minutes or until the mixture thickens.

Strain through a sieve and pour the mixture into the tart shell. Allow to cool slightly, then refrigerate for 1 hour or until set.

SERVES 8

SKINNY MINNIE BROWNIES

SUGAR-FREE | VEGETARIAN | 536 KJ/128 CAL PER SERVE

1 teaspoon olive oil, for greasing

350 g (12¾ oz/1 cup) honey or maple syrup, or 250 ml (9 fl oz/1 cup) rice malt syrup

40 g (1½ oz/⅓ cup) unsweetened cocoa or cacao powder

75 g (2¾ oz/½ cup) plain (all-purpose) flour

¼ teaspoon baking powder

¼ teaspoon bicarbonate of soda (baking soda)

¼ teaspoon salt

135 g (4¾ oz/½ cup) unsweetened apple sauce

2 tablespoons coconut oil (or olive oil)

2 teaspoons natural vanilla extract

1 egg (free-range, organic), at room temperature

60 g (2¼ oz/½ cup) chopped walnuts or pecans (optional)

85 g (3 oz/½ cup) semisweet chocolate chips or cacao nibs (optional)

Preheat the oven to 180°C (350°F). Line a 20 cm (8 inch) baking tin with baking paper and lightly spray with olive oil.

Measure the honey into a large bowl and microwave on high for 45 seconds. Whisk in the cocoa and allow to cool.

Meanwhile, in a small bowl, combine the flour, baking powder, bicarbonate of soda and salt.

In a large bowl, whisk the apple sauce, coconut oil and vanilla together until well combined. (Note: if you need to smooth out the coconut oil, heat it in the microwave for 10 seconds.)

Add the egg, then the cooled honey-cocoa mixture, nuts and choc chips (or cacao nibs, if using) and stir until smooth. Add the flour mixture and stir until all the flour is incorporated. Pour into the baking tin and spread out evenly.

Bake for 25–30 minutes. It's important not to overbake the mixture. To test it, insert a toothpick into the centre. It's ready if there are a few moist crumbs on it.

Cool the mixture in the tin on a wire rack. Remove the brownies using the baking paper and slice into 16 squares.

MAKES 16

GUILT-FREE HONEYCOMB

DAIRY-FREE | GLUTEN-FREE | NUT-FREE | VEGETARIAN | 130–163 KJ/31–39 CAL PER SERVE

110 g (3¾ oz / ½ cup) sugar, or 50 g (1¾ oz) stevia

4 tablespoons honey, or maple syrup or golden syrup

1½ teaspoons bicarbonate of soda (baking soda)

Line a baking tray with baking paper and have it close at hand.

In a large saucepan, bring the sugar and honey to a low boil and cook until the mixture is a golden colour.

As soon as it is a golden caramel colour, immediately remove from the heat and, working quickly and carefully (because hot caramel can burn you), add the bicarbonate of soda.

Stir the bicarbonate of soda in quickly; it will immediately froth. Pour it at once into the prepared tray. Let it cool at room temperature until it hardens, then break it into pieces and store in an airtight container.

MAKES 20–25 PIECES

tips

This recipe has simple ingredients but timing is a big factor and a mere matter of seconds can make the difference between honeycomb and a sticky mess. Here are our tried and tested tips:
- Boil the sugar on a very low temperature.
- It can take 12–15 minutes to become golden.
- Don't stir the sugar mixture more than once or twice at most.
- Honeycomb hates a wet or humid environment: water is basically the demise of honeycomb … so make it on a dry, cool day.

FAUXNUTS 4 WAYS

DONUTS

2 teaspoons butter, for greasing

28 g (1 oz/¼ cup) coconut flour

30 g (1 oz/¼ cup) unsweetened cocoa or cacao powder, plus 1 tablespoon stevia (for chocolate donuts)

1 tablespoon natural vanilla extract (for vanilla donuts)

¼ teaspoon salt

¼ teaspoon bicarbonate of soda (baking soda)

½ teaspoon ground cinnamon (for vanilla donuts)

4 eggs (free-range, organic)

80 ml (2½ fl oz/⅓ cup) coconut oil

80 ml (2½ fl oz/⅓ cup) maple syrup or 125 ml (4 fl oz/½ cup) rice malt syrup

Preheat the oven to 175°C (345°F). Grease a donut pan or a muffin tin generously.

In a food processor, combine the coconut flour, cocoa mixture for the chocolate fauxnuts or vanilla for the vanilla fauxnuts, salt, bicarbonate of soda and cinnamon (if using) and pulse to combine. Add the eggs, coconut oil and maple syrup (or rice malt syrup, if using) and pulse until well combined.

Fill each donut well or muffin hole to halfway with the batter. Use a spatula to even out the batter.

Bake for 15 minutes or until a toothpick inserted in a donut comes out clean. Remove from the oven and allow to cool in the pan for 5 minutes, then tip out onto a wire rack to cool completely before adding glaze.

If you are using a muffin pan, then use a knife or a small cookie cutter to cut a hole in the centre of each donut.

MAKES 8

GF | NF | SF | V
1402 KJ/335 CAL PER SERVE

CHOCOLATE COCONUT GLAZE

30 g (1 oz/¼ cup) unsweetened cocoa or cacao powder

125 ml (4 fl oz/¼ cup) coconut oil

30 g (1 oz/½ cup) coconut flakes

In a small bowl, whisk together the cocoa or cacao and coconut oil until well combined. Carefully dunk the top of each donut into the chocolate mixture. Sprinkle with coconut flakes, then put them in the fridge for up to 5 minutes to allow the chocolate glaze to harden.

GF | SF | V
1402 KJ/335 CAL PER SERVE

MAPLE GLAZE

80 g (2¾ oz/½ cup) cashews

60 ml (2 fl oz/¼ cup) maple syrup or 170 ml (5¾ fl oz/⅔ cup) rice malt syrup

80 ml (2½ fl oz/⅓ cup) coconut oil

2 tablespoons water

Combine all of the ingredients in a blender and process until smooth and creamy. If it's too thick to pour, add more water, a tiny bit at a time. Pour into a shallow bowl and dip the top of each donut into the glaze. Return to the wire rack.

GF | NF | SF | V
1255 KJ/300 CAL PER SERVE

STRAWBERRY GLAZE

125 ml (4 fl oz/½ cup) coconut oil

¼ teaspoon natural vanilla extract

pinch of sea salt

75 g (2¾ oz/½ cup) fresh strawberries, hulled

whipped cream (optional), to serve

Combine all of the ingredients in a food processor or blender. Pulse until it is puréed and uniformly pink. Pour the glaze into a shallow bowl. Dip each donut in the glaze, then chill in the fridge for a few minutes or until the glaze hardens. If the glaze is not thin enough, warm it slightly to liquefy the coconut oil. Serve with whipped cream if desired.

GF | SF | V
1205 KJ/288 CAL PER SERVE

CARAMEL GLAZE

175 g (6 oz/½ cup) honey or 255 ml (8½ fl oz/¾ cup) rice malt syrup

1½ tablespoons almond spread

3 teaspoons butter

½ teaspoon natural vanilla extract

35 g (1¼ oz/¼ cup) sliced almonds, to sprinkle

In a small saucepan over medium heat, bring the honey to a low boil. Simmer for 8–10 minutes or until it is a deep golden colour.

Remove from the heat and add the almond spread, butter and vanilla. Let it cool. Dip the top of each donut in the glaze, then sprinkle with sliced almonds.

MUM'S CHOCOLATE TART WITH SALT FLAKES

NUT-FREE | VEGETARIAN | 2607 KJ/623 CAL PER SERVE

1 sheet frozen shortcrust pastry, thawed (or a store-bought pastry tart shell, optional)

300 ml (10½ fl oz/1½ cups) thick (double) cream

2 teaspoons caster (superfine) sugar or stevia

pinch of sea salt

50 g (1¾ oz) unsalted butter, softened

300 g (10½ oz) dark chocolate, broken into small pieces, or 300 g (10½ oz) cacao nibs

pink salt flakes, to decorate

125 ml (4 fl oz/½ cup) thick (double) cream mixed with 125 g (4½ oz/½ cup) sour cream, to serve

---

CLEAN VERSION

200 g (8 oz/2 cups) almond flour
pinch of sea salt
2 tablespoons coconut oil
1 egg (free-range, organic)

To make your own pastry, pulse the flour and salt in a food processor until combined. Add the coconut oil and egg, mixing until you achieve a dough-like consistency (it usually becomes a ball shape). Press the dough into the tart tin and trim any excess. Blind bake as per the method above.

Preheat the oven to 180°C (350°F).

Grease and line a 20 cm (8 inch) tart tin. Lay the pastry sheet in the tin and trim any excess. Cover the pastry base with baking paper, fill with dried beans or ceramic baking beans and blind bake for 10–15 minutes. Remove the beans and bake for another 15 minutes or until golden.

While the pastry is cooking, put the cream, sugar (or stevia, if using) and salt in a saucepan and bring it to the boil. Remove from the heat as soon as the mixture boils, then add the butter and chocolate pieces (or cacao nibs, if using). Stir until completely melted and blended and the mixture is glossy.

Pour into the tart shell and stand at room temperature for 3–4 hours or until set, or refrigerate until firm.

Sprinkle salt flakes lightly all over. In a small bowl, fold together the thick cream and sour cream and serve on the side.

SERVES 8

TIP

Our mum made this recipe for us when we were growing up, albeit without the salt flakes: that's our addition! This was her Saturday night dinner party go-to recipe. We love it because it's quick and always delivers a 'wow'. We've not only added the salt flakes but we've also cleaned up the original version for an optional healthier spin on this treat.

MEAL PLANS

We all live busy lives, so to make life just that little bit easier, we've pulled together some suggested weekly meal plans for you. The plans are designed to give you a broad range of nutrients, thanks to lean proteins, superfoods and vegies. We've also given you as much variety as possible across each week so that you won't get bored. The best part? We've included dessert EVERY day! Woo hoo! The daily calorie count comes in at

	MONDAY	TUESDAY	WEDNESDAY
BREAKFAST	Choc Berry Fix Smoothie (page 73)	Easy Overnight Oats (page 55)	Rustic Tomato & Spinach Scrambled Eggs (page 56)
LUNCH	Superfood Supersalad (page 116)	Chicken, Kale & Lemon Soup (page 120)	Salmon Carpaccio (page 91)
DINNER	Seared Beef Carpaccio with Olive & Tomato Tapenade (page 158)	No Noodle Pad Thai (page 132)	Quick Chicken Lettuce Wraps (page 139)
DESSERT	Dark Chocolate & Date Fro-Yo Bark (page 226)	No-Bake Coconut Bars (page 237)	Raw Caramel Apple Pie (page 238)

the GOOD life

around 6276 kilojoules (1500 calories), including dessert. If you are on a weight-loss diet and skip dessert, then most days will come in under 5020 kilojoules (1200 calories). Either way, you're getting the benefit of a diet filled with essential vitamins, nutrients, healthy fats and heaps of flavour. *Bon appétit!*

THURSDAY	FRIDAY	SATURDAY	SUNDAY
Cauli Crush Smoothie (page 72)	Kale & Bean Jumble (page 38)	Banana Bread (page 30)	Lemon & Thyme Haloumi on Olive Sourdough (page 22)
Asparagus & Ricotta Tart (page 96)	Chicken Udon Noodle Soup (page 95)	Zucchini Noodles with Tomato & Feta (page 89)	Lick the Plate Lamb Souvlaki (page 124)
Seared Beef with Soba Noodle Salad (page 131)	15-Minute Prawn Curry (page 154)	Sticky Spiced Duck (page 144) Serve with Super Green Slaw (page 180)	Spicy Broccoli Soup (page 173)
Vanilla Banana Nice Cream (page 233)	Fudge Fix (page 256)	Minty Pink Grapefruit Granita (page 242)	Raspberry Vanilla Popsicles (page 248)

MEAL PLANS

	MONDAY	TUESDAY	WEDNESDAY
BREAKFAST	Chocolate Chia Pudding (page 41)	Superfood Smoothie Bowl (page 48)	Baby Bok Choy Frittata (page 68)
LUNCH	Bean & Feta Salad with Fresh Mint (page 198)	Brussels Sprouts Salad (page 201)	Lime & Basil Prawns (page 76)
DINNER	Sticky Lamb Ribs (page 157) Serve with mixed greens	Chicken & Leek Pie (page 147)	Skillet Lasagne (page 136)
DESSERT	Cheesecake with Berry Coulis (page 245)	Super Quick Coconut Choc (page 241)	Raspberry Nice Cream (page 233)

WEEK 2

THURSDAY	FRIDAY	SATURDAY	SUNDAY
Labneh & Fig Tartine (page 60)	Pine Lime Smoothie (page 73)	Lean Life Smoothie (page 72)	Skillet Baked Eggs (page 63)
Rainbow Silverbeet with Slivered Almonds (page 123)	Chicken San Choy Bow (page 103)	Super Filling Brunch Bowl (page 21)	Fig & Buffalo Mozzarella Salad (page 192)
Seared Steak with Chimichurri (page 151) Serve with Sweet Potato Chips with Chilli (page 214)	Cauliflower Crust Pizza (page 128)	Salt & Pepper Prawns (page 148) Serve with Kale Salad with Preserved Lemon (page 202)	Lemon & Herb Roast Chicken (page 162)
Blueberry Bliss Fro-Yo Bark (page 226)	Individual Raspberry & Chocolate Puddings (page 251)	Chocolate Nice Cream (page 233)	Rhubarb & Vanilla Pie (page 234)

MEAL PLANS

	MONDAY	TUESDAY	WEDNESDAY
BREAKFAST	Going Nuts Granola (page 26)	Raspberry Chia Pudding (page 41)	The ABC Smoothie Bowl (page 48)
LUNCH	Asian Chicken Noodle Salad (page 107)	Watercress Soup (page 83)	Zucchini Noodles with Avocado Pesto (page 88)
DINNER	Fab Fish Fajitas (page 165)	Roast Harissa Chicken (page 143) Serve with Kale Salad with Preserved Lemon (page 202)	Quick Sticks Ginger Beef (page 140)
DESSERT	Mango & Coconut Popsicle (page 248)	2-Minute Chocolate Mug Cake (page 230)	Skinny Minnie Brownies (page 260)

the GOOD *life*

WEEK 3

THURSDAY	FRIDAY	SATURDAY	SUNDAY
3-Ingredient Scrambled Eggs (page 25)	Energy Elixir Smoothie (page 72)	Turkish Eggs with Sumac Yoghurt (page 18)	Coco-Vanilla Pancakes (page 33)
One-Pot Quinoa & Kale Pilaf (page 205)	Thai Chopped Chicken Salad with Chilli Dressing (page 107)	Tomato & Ricotta Crustless Torte (page 79)	Chia-Seared Tuna with Rainbow Salad (page 84)
Sticky Salmon with Ribbon Salad (page 169)	Chickpea & Vegie Curry (page 166)	Whole Baked Snapper with Salsa Verde (page 135) Serve with mixed greens	Slow-Cooked Pork Burritos with Corn Salsa (page 174)
Guilt-Free Honeycomb (page 263)	Salted Date Caramel Nice Cream (page 233)	Vanilla Panna Cotta with Figs & Honey (page 255)	Lean & Luscious Yoghurt & Berry Tart (page 252)

INDEX

the GOOD *life*

INDEX

the GOOD *life*

INDEX

the GOOD life

INDEX

the GOOD life

CONNECT WITH US

We'd love for you to check in with us at **SWIISH.com**, and subscribe for new recipes, videos, tips, tricks, giveaways and lots more.

You can also find us:

On Instagram **@swiishbysallyo**

On Twitter at **twitter.com/swiishbysallyo**

On Facebook at **facebook.com/swiishbysallyobermeder**

Don't forget to tag SWIISH in your snaps, selfies and healthies (healthy selfies!), and share your favourite recipes with us.

Connect with Sally Obermeder:

On Instagram **@sallyobermeder**

On Twitter at **twitter.com/sallyobermeder**

On Facebook at **facebook.com/sallyobermeder**

Connect with Maha Koraiem:

On Instagram **@maha_koraiem**

On Twitter at **twitter.com/maha_koraiem**

On Facebook at **facebook.com/maha.koraiem**

the GOOD life

Never Stop Believing

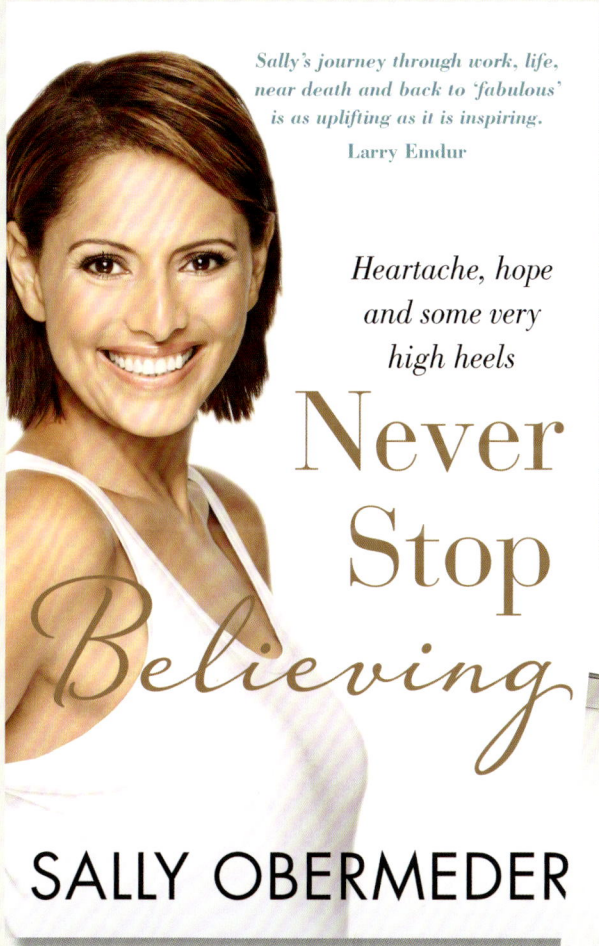

Sally's journey through work, life, near death and back to 'fabulous' is as uplifting as it is inspiring.
Larry Emdur

Heartache, hope and some very high heels

Never Stop Believing

SALLY OBERMEDER

super green smoothies

'Your daily go-to guide and new best friend in the kitchen.'
James Duigan,
Celebrity Trainer

AUSTRALIA'S
#1
BESTSELLING
SMOOTHIE BOOK

SALLY OBERMEDER & MAHA KORAIEM

60 delicious recipes for weight loss, energy and vitality

NOW AVAILABLE IN BOOKSHOPS AND ALSO ONLINE AS EBOOKS

THANK YOU

Thank you to everyone in our lives who has supported our many roles and the different things we do—whether it's TV or our website, businesses and charity commitments. You've been part of it all, unwavering in tough times and in good. You drive us to be the best we can be.

To our SWIISH.com community—you've been part of our lives and our story from the day we started. We could never have predicted that what seemed like a small venture would explode the way it has. We have grown as a tribe and along the way so many more have joined us. We are so humbled and grateful.

To everyone who bought *Super Green Smoothies* and loved it, and who became so passionate about adopting a super green lifestyle, we can't thank you enough. You've stopped us in the street (and we love it!), flooded us with emails and shared your Instagram and Facebook posts, telling us about your weight loss and increased energy as well as the turnaround in your lives as a result of adopting *Super Green Smoothies*.

This book is thanks to you guys, who wanted more and kept asking us for more. Nothing delights and inspires us more than being part of your health and wellbeing journeys.

To our parents, and to Margitta and Manfred—thank you all for your endless love and support with everything we do. Mum, thank you for being an incredible cook, for passing down your recipes through our family and for teaching us that cooking is all about love. We love you all so much!

From Sal, to Marcus and Annabelle—you are the loves of my life. Thank you for believing in me—I couldn't love you more if I tried.

To everyone who worked with us on this book—you know who you are—thank you all for your commitment, passion and energy. We are so grateful.